M000073821

YOU
CAN BE
YOURSELF
HERE

YOU CAN BE YOURSELF HERE

YOUR POCKET GUIDE TO CREATING INCLUSIVE WORKPLACES
BY USING THE PSYCHOLOGY OF BELONGING

DDS DOBSON-SMITH

LIONCREST
PUBLISHING

Copyright © 2022 DDS Dobson-Smith

All rights reserved.

YOU CAN BE YOURSELF HERE

*Your Pocket Guide to Creating Inclusive Workplaces
by Using the Psychology of Belonging*

ISBN 978-1-5445-2654-6 *Paperback*

978-1-5445-2655-3 *Ebook*

978-1-5445-2700-0 *Audiobook*

Before I continue, I would like to dedicate this book to
the brave and beautiful people who continue to show up as themselves
despite the inexorable pressure from the world to be someone else.

To my teachers, you inspire me.
If it weren't for you, I would not be me:

Aaron Reardon, Adisa Stewart, Aishah Iqbal, Aisling Farrell,
Amanda Schmidt, Amit Verma, Andrew Stinger, Angus Jenkins,
Anna Benassi, Anna Menitti, Ashley Williams, Austin Sherman,
Aysa Kirschner, Benjamin Farrand, Bethanie Jayne Beardmore,
Briana Lyndon, Brittany Mullan, Cat Bilski,
Catherine Sharp-Aouchiche, Cathy Carl, Charlie Chapin,
Charlie Sample, Chelsea True, Dr. Chris Shambrook, CJ, Claire Libbey,
Courtney Reynolds, Cyndi Case, Dan Sullivan, Danny Schnittman,
David Dobson-Smith, Dawn Barker, Dean Rubinstein,
DeAngela Cooks, Dr. Dennis Reno, Dino Gossens-Larson,
Dock Fox, elle black, Elissa Grey, Emma Harris, Emily Abramson,
Emily Marinelli, Erin Howe, Gesshin Greenwood,
Dr. George Kitahara Kich, Dr. Gabri Gherbaz, Galina, Goujon,
Gary Hirthler, Gina Amaro Rudan, Dr. Gregory Desierto,
Gwen Watson, Heather Buchheim, Heather Emmerzael,

Holly St. Clair Moor, Irem Cavusoglu, Jay Louie, Jason Beiley,
Jay Tzvia Helfland, Jeff Huang, Jennifer Remling, Jenny Likansis,
Jessica Joseph, Jessica Pourhassanian, Joey Konkel, Jon Caña,
Jonny Morris, Josh Bareño, Juan Cortés, Jude McCormack,
Kalpita Patel, Kate Moriarty, Katie Farber, Katie DeBoer,
Karen 'Treacle' Jones, Kaycie Crossley, Keith Hatter, Kristin Parris,
Kyoko Matsushita, Lauren Feig, Lindsey Wells, Dr. Ling Lam,
Dr. Liz Abrams, Mackenzie Studebaker, Mandy Walis, Marcus Powell,
Maria Athena Bughao, Matt Barker, Mary Beth Schuler, MJ Morrissey,
MK Hurlbutt, Neil Sharp, Dr. Nick Bustos, Nick Corrigan,
Nick Walker, Nisha Nizaam, Paul Emerich France, Pilar Prime,
Quinn Case, Rachael Brooke Hoppock, Rachael Vaughan,
Sarah Frances, Sarita Baker, Sean Miller, Dr. Seth Pardo,
Scott Larson, Shane Murphy, Shiva Wilson, Stephanie Bain,
Taunya Black, Thomas Thiel, Tiffinity Bodderfly, Tim J. Newman,
Valerie Todd, Veli Aghdiran, Vicki Williams, and Wega Bratsch.

And to my clients and patients who, for confidentiality,
will remain unnamed here but not unacknowledged.
Thank you for showing me the way.

CONTENTS

INTRODUCTION

I f you're reading this book, it is highly likely that you survived high school.

I use the term "survived" quite deliberately because high school is a nearly universal experience: a gauntlet of tumultuous times as you are either entering or coming out of puberty, so your hormones are doing some pretty messed-up things to make you feel weird, awkward, and out of place. The prevailing developmental quest that happens while we are at high school is that of finding your own identity and of attempting to individuate from your parents while at the same time endeavoring to fit in with everyone else. And in our quest to fit in, we learn to code switch, cover up aspects of our identity, bend ourselves into different shapes, and engage in a plethora of unworkable and ultimately futile behaviors in order to belong.

High school is marked by so many challenging and potentially traumatic experiences of being singled out by teachers, not being able to kick a ball high enough, or, hell, having to undress and shower in front of everyone after PE. This all becomes amplified if you are Black, Brown, or mixed-race, if you are female, trans, or queer, or if you are disabled in some way. For any human being at that age, it's a time of change and turmoil. If you're also a person who comes from a historically disempowered or oppressed community, it's even worse.

Sometimes, it probably felt like you were never going to survive that area of your life…but you did!

However, surviving doesn't mean that the experience wasn't terrible or that you no longer bear the scars from it. So, when you go on to encounter situations that are similar enough to those experiences you dealt with in high school, all of those memories and feelings resurface and are brought into the present day. Without being aware of it, we respond to here-and-now experiences with there-and-then programming.

Let me share with you a personal story by way of illustrating my point. As an overweight, queer teen, I was desperate to find my people. I tried to fit in with the boys, the girls, the sporty kids (definitely didn't work), the geeky kids, the naughty kids

—I even tried to fit in with the teachers and the dinner ladies.[1] To do so, I would disown or suppress an aspect of my Self,[2] my behavior, or my personality in order to be deemed acceptable by others so that they would not "other" me.[3] These acts were ultimately futile because that which was suppressed will eventually became expressed, leading to my newfound community backing away from the person they thought they knew and rendering me alone to live out my status as an outsider who could be bullied and picked on.

When I was fourteen years old, I had an English Literature class with Mr. Neville. After one assignment, he threw my essay back at me and said, "Dobson-Smith, you need to be more like Rachel Warner. She has written an amazing essay."

The class laughed at me, I felt shamed, and (in that moment, at least) I hated Rachel Warner—and I despised Mr. Neville.

---

[1] "Dinner ladies" is a term used by, and for, the (mostly) women who were employed by my school to cook and serve lunch, and to monitor and look after students during lunch breaks.

[2] The capital S on the word "Self" is deliberate and speaks to a body of work by Heinz Kohut called *Self Psychology*, which will be explored in Chapter I.

[3] Othering is the action of viewing or treating a person or group of people as intrinsically different from and alien to oneself.

Fast-forward a couple of decades, and somebody in a professional context said to me, "DDS, you should go and speak to this person who can help you improve on this area of work."

On one level, that was a perfectly innocuous expression of help that person was trying to give me. But on another level, I immediately thought, *Holy hell, I am* not *going to do that!*

I remembered the shame I felt when Mr. Neville told me that I wasn't as good as Rachel Warner, so there was no way I was going to go and ask for help. My there-and-then programming fueled my knee-jerk reaction, even though there was no direct relation to the here-and-now situation I was in.

This book is not about healing the scars from surviving high school; it's about acknowledging our need for inclusion and recognizing that certain elements of the workplace are similar enough to high school that they can bring forward, trigger, and emulate some of the feelings of exclusion and awkwardness we felt back then.

Think about it: there are many parallels between high school and the world of work. Classes have become departments; principals and headteachers have become CEOs; the administration has become shareholders or boards of directors; and the teenage cliques, factions, groups, and gangs have transformed into "those you lunch with"—and those you don't.

I SEE YOUR PAIN

Because you have picked up this book, I would imagine you are worried about high levels of attrition and low levels of satisfaction amongst your employees, particularly within historically disempowered and marginalized communities.

Beyond the data, you probably have firsthand experience of the challenges people are experiencing in terms of belonging in your workplace. Perhaps you've noticed cliques forming amongst certain groups of colleagues. Maybe you are dealing with an increasing number of employee grievances about microaggressions and exclusionary behavior.[4] Or it could be that you have started to become aware of how few candidates you are able to attract, hire, and keep from underrepresented communities.

You might be feeling the pressure to come up with a plan to evolve the culture, stem the attrition tide, and boost morale,

---

[4] Microaggression: A statement, action, or incident regarded as an instance of indirect, subtle, or unintentional discrimination against members of a marginalized group, such as a racial or ethnic minority.

but you are at a loss as to where to start because of the overwhelming size of the problem.

And then, there is your own experience of belonging.

These dynamics and their parallels to high school can be at best a distraction and at worst damaging. They impact the performance of individuals, teams, and organizations in unseen and powerful ways. I have come to appreciate over the years—and through my work around the globe—that belonging is an archetypal experience that we all seek. It transcends geographies, cultures, and identities.

I also sense that, while my experience of belonging is just that—my experience—I'm not alone in my experiences of not-belonging in places I wished I did, and I'm not alone in my quest for finding belonging in places that I should.

MY STORY

I grew up in a small town. I was overweight, struggling to come terms with being queer, and living in a home where I was verbally, mentally, and emotionally abused and neglected. Love was conditional, and I don't truly know what it feels like to be nurtured by a primary caregiver. The only times I received any positive attention were when I performed well on a test, vacuumed the carpet, or made a sandwich for my dad.

I always felt like I had to change who I was to become acceptable (and, therefore, accepted) and to find a place where I would be included and welcomed. I was bullied and ostracized in my own social environment, just as many people are in high school.

My journey to belonging was a series of happenings, but the very first time I felt like I belonged was when I was working at Marks & Spencer (a British retailer) as a personnel management trainee in Cardiff, Wales. The store manager at the time, a guy called Paul Smith, pulled me to one side and said to me, "I see you. I see you trying to be something you're not, and I want to help you."

He helped me to access company-sponsored therapy sessions—it was the first time I'd ever been to therapy.

That was when I was twenty-four years old. I'm now forty-eight, as of the writing of this book, so that was half my life ago. Today, I'm a published author, an executive coach, a speaker on leadership and growth—and a licensed therapist. It was the conversation with Paul Smith—that intervention, that amount of care and love from somebody who was several ranks senior to me, noticing and deciding to help—that was the catalyst that shifted my own career trajectory.

Of course, the journey from then to now is never a straight line.

In my adult life, I came out as gay (I now identify as queer, but back then "queer" was a derogatory term) and then found myself in three abusive relationships, repeating what I had learned earlier in life. It wasn't until I met David, now my husband who I've been with for sixteen years, that I began to realize that I could be loved for who I am—just as I am.

From that moment when we met when I was thirty-one years old, I have worked to undo all of what I learned to be false about myself. I spent the first half of my life learning that it wasn't okay to be me, and I have spent the second half of my life (so far) discovering that, actually, it is more than okay to be who I am. It is *glorious* to be me.

I know that when I like being me, and when I can be me without fear of being shunned or rejected from the group I'm in, I feel fantastic. I sleep better, I treat myself better, and I feel more alive. I feel more motivated, so I can bring all of myself to my work and be creative, innovative, daring, present—and just *better*.

BUT WHAT DOES THIS HAVE
TO DO WITH YOU?

As I mentioned earlier, while my specific stories are unique to me, my overall experience is a more universal one.

I have spent over twenty-five years working in corporations, in areas of organizational development, learning and development, and cultural transformation, in addition to becoming a therapist, an executive coach, and a Reiki master. Becoming and doing all these things has been in service of helping other people grow and become who they are.

When you are your you-est you, the best version of yourself, then everything about your life becomes gorgeous.

Time and time again, in my coaching practice, in my therapy practice, and in my social world, I have seen that when we welcome all parts of ourselves in, we are magnificent. And when we are magnificent, there is more of ourselves available to our work, our customers, and our relationships. It is only when we like ourselves that we can begin to feel like we belong.

When we're still trying to fit in, we tend to "cover," a phenomenon generally experienced by anybody who has an aspect of their identity that doesn't come from the dominant group. If you are female-bodied, Black or Brown, LGBTQIA2+[5]—if you have any aspect of your identity that is not white, straight, cis-gender, male, able-bodied, middle-class, attractive, thin—then you experience oppression and marginalization. As a result, we try to cover up those aspects. When mothers go to work, they don't talk about their children because they think it will limit their promotional opportunities. Queer people don't want to talk about their same-sex relationships, or people who don't drink don't want to go to work events because they have to explain why they're not having a beer. So you cover, suppressing aspects of your identity—of who you are—in order to be deemed acceptable by the others, whoever the others are.

When you are finally deemed acceptable by the others, they will then include you. And when you are included, you feel like you belong. And when you feel like you belong, you can therefore let more of yourself show.

But there are a couple of problems with that. First, as you let more of yourself show, the people who have accepted the suppressed or covered version of you start to see these new aspects. They think, *Well, you're not who we thought you were*, and they start to move away from you. The other problem

---

[5] Lesbian, Gay, Bisexual, Transgender, Queer, Questioning, Intersex, Asexual, 2-Spirit.

with covering and suppressing aspects of your identity is that it takes an astronomical amount of internal energy to be someone that you're not. And that energy that goes toward remembering who you are to certain people in certain environments is energy taken away from your own performance and delivery at work.

So, when you can be in a workplace where you don't have to cover or suppress, you have more energy available for performance, for work, for being there for your clients.

While I, of course, want you to feel like your best *you*, this is a book about belonging in the workplace. First, you must belong; then, you can begin to foster a culture of belonging within your organization.

DIVERSITY + INCLUSION = BELONGING

But what *is* belonging? And how does it relate to the buzzwords we've all seen have a massive uptick in recent years: diversity and inclusion?

The words diversity and inclusion are often used not only in the same sentence, but in the same breath. While they are definitely relatives, I would say they are more like cousins than they are siblings. When spoken about as if they were synonymous, it leads us to ignore, or forget, the distinct role each plays in the creation of the emotional experience of belonging.

A wise colleague of mine recently said to me, "Diversity is a fact. Inclusion is a behavior. Belonging is a feeling." While I mostly agree with her, I would exchange the last word "feeling" with *experience*.

Diversity is a fact in that you can you look around and ask, "Am I amongst people who are like me?" Yes, great. "And are there other people who are *not* like me?" Yes again? Then you have diversity. You either have diversity or you do not, particularly in the world of work, based on the demographics of the workforce. So, it's a fact: either your organization is or is not diverse.

Inclusion is a set of behaviors, frameworks, or approaches whereby you are able to leverage a diverse workforce by ensuring that the diversity is being used, invited, and welcomed. That their voices are heard. That people with historically disempowered identities are given power and have an equitable seat at the table. Those are the behaviors of inclusion.

Belonging is an experience that can only happen when you have both diversity and inclusion. If there is diversity in the workplace *and* there are inclusive behaviors, then it is likely that you will feel belonging in that workplace.

Thus, diversity plus inclusion equals belonging, but diversity doesn't always lead to inclusion if you don't have all of the component parts.

If you don't have diversity, you walk into a place and encounter a sea of whiteness or straightness or whatever the dominant feature is. *But*, you think, *we can recruit diversity*. Well, without existing diversity, people from underrepresented communities won't be attracted to your organization. But let's say that your recruitment team does a really great job of hiring people from diverse backgrounds. When they start at the organization, if there aren't inclusive policies, practices, and behaviors amongst the leaders and within the organizational infrastructure, then they won't feel like they belong and they won't stay.

The absence of the experience of belonging is what causes low morale and high attrition.

But the opposite is also true: if you have hired diversity into the organization, you've created a diverse workforce, and you do have policies, practices, and behaviors that drive inclusion, it becomes highly likely that employees will experience a feeling of belonging. And when they feel like they belong, they will stay. In fact, they will be happy to stay, and they will be able to deliver their best because they're not covering an aspect of themselves.

WHY I'M WRITING THIS BOOK

Everyone—no matter what body they were born into, no matter where they come from, no matter what they believe—deserves to belong. I believe that the experience of belonging has never been more desired, yet has never been more at risk, especially in the world of work. I know, from personal experience, what it takes to build workplaces where people experience belonging —and the magic that happens when they do.

I have seen time and again, the world over, that when human beings feel like they belong somewhere, the psychological resources (that would otherwise be preoccupied in helping that person to bend themselves out of shape to fit in) are liberated to focus on what's important: their performance, their work, and their relationships.

I am writing this book to help you create the conditions for your people to do just that. By reading this book, you will learn about:

- The psychology of belonging and its impact on workplace performance

- How to create a culture of belonging in your workplace

- Practical tips for tackling issues of diversity and facilitating inclusion

- Real-life "tales from the field" about people's personal experiences of belonging (or lack thereof) at work

During the summer of 2020, I interviewed people about their experience of belonging in the workplace. Every person I interviewed spoke, in their own words, to the presence or absence of the psychological aspects of belonging that you will learn about in the next chapter. Each of them described the ways in which the presence or absence of the experience of belonging had either positively or negatively impacted their performance. I hope these stories, which open and close each chapter, will provide further credence to the importance of belonging in the workplace, along with additional examples of how workplaces can facilitate the experience for their employees.

BEFORE WE BEGIN

Let's face it: the 2020s did not get off to the greatest of starts.

Putting aside for one moment the paradigm-shifting, life-changing, global COVID-19 pandemic, 2020, at least in America, was a year of uprising in response to social injustice experienced by the Black community. While the murders of George Floyd and Breonna Taylor (amongst many others) received significant media attention (and sparked months of protests and riots), theirs were just two of 1,100 lives lost annually to police violence, a disproportionate number of which come from the Black community.

Additionally, 2019 marked the fiftieth anniversary of the Stonewall Riots and the beginning of the LGBTQIA2+ Rights Movement, and even though homosexuality was de-pathologized in 1973, the march toward equality for the community continues. For example, in 2020, the US government tabled legislation that would walk back protections for LGBTQIA2+ people and allow hospitals to turn them away. This happened in the midst of the global COVID-19 pandemic, and in the words of Bre Kidman, a nonbinary candidate who ran for the US Senate in Maine, "I'm scared to say this out loud, but I'm afraid that trans people will face things like being deprioritized for ventilators or for care." This is just one example of the everyday threat of losing basic human rights that the LGBTQIA2+ community faces in America today.

Relatedly, in 2006, Tarana Burke, a social activist and community organizer, began using the phrase "Me Too" on the Myspace social network to promote "empowerment through empathy" among women of color who have been sexually abused. But it wouldn't be until 2017, when more than eighty women made allegations against Harvey Weinstein, an American movie producer, that her words would spark the #MeToo social media campaign leading to many similar sexual abuse allegations against (and dismissals of) powerful men around the world.

I share these examples of inequality and marginalization on the basis of gender, sexuality, and race to remind you that even though the topics of diversity, inclusion, and belonging are currently high on the agenda, they are not new issues. They are also not the only issues of oppression and marginalization that loom large and present barriers to belonging for people on an everyday basis. In a world that favors and gives an automatic leg up to anyone who is white/light-skinned, male, straight, cisgender, able-bodied, middle-to-upper class, middle-aged, or thin, it's clear that we've got work to do.

I want to be clear that this book is not a political statement about red versus blue, Republican versus Democrat, or Tory versus Labor. At the same time, I want to acknowledge that it is not possible to have a conversation about equality and equity without, at some point, also talking about structural oppression and the way in which legal and political systems work to keep said structural oppression in place and alive.

With all of that said, this book is written in support of the human experience and the steps you can take, regardless of political affiliation, to create intentional workplaces where people feel like they belong.

CHAPTER 1

THE PSYCHOLOGY
OF BELONGING

*"Our goal in life is to
become increasingly better at being
at odds with ourselves."*

—DR. CARL BUCHHEIT

D D is an Asian-American, queer, nonbinary person in their early forties who lives and works in San Francisco, California.

I WORK AT A PRESCHOOL-THROUGH-EIGHTH-GRADE independent school with a diverse population—diverse ethnically (at about 49 percent BIPOC and 51 percent white); socioeconomically (with 42 percent of the school population on a sliding scale of tuition support); and relationally (with 38 percent of the school population who are LGBTQIA+, a number of students, families, and staff who are nonbinary or trans, and many students coming from single-parent or multi-household home lives). I work in a company that has:

- Clear systems and structures that are actively working to employ and support people and families of all backgrounds and makeup.

- A clearly articulated stance on community and anti-racist/anti-bias allyship.

- Roles that support the work that is considered essential—multiple roles in and outside the classroom for coaches and mentors around community and belonging.

- Active work as a community to understand and engage with the sense of belonging and how authenticity and vulnerability play essential roles in our work.

I have always been high-achieving and mission-aligned. This is the first organization I have worked for where I feel like I can be all of me.

Throughout most of my career in education, spanning nearly twenty years, being myself—*all* of myself—has not been encouraged. I certainly never felt comfortable being fully me. I have been told not to share my sexuality, to be less of this or more like that. I experienced microaggressions aplenty during that time; people made jokes and offhand comments right in front of me.

I remember one school that I worked at told me to "tone it down," because we wouldn't want to upset families and we don't know what the children might be sharing when they go home. What does that even mean?! That was never really defined to me. Just stop being me and be less— shine less brightly, put on a mask that is reflective of the community, and stay in my swim lane.

Even worse was the realization that opportunities for professional growth and development were simply not accessible to me.

This experience was disheartening and bad for my self-worth and self-esteem. I used alcohol to cope with the unhappiness I felt. I would leave work as soon as it ended, or I would work excessively to "prove my worth." It wasn't until recently that I realized the impact my time at that particular school has had on me at a personal and trauma level. It reignited things that I have been told my whole life and made me shrink even further into what I believed I needed to be to be successful.

Eventually, I moved schools and got away from that environment. With each move, I allowed myself to be more open about who I am—and who I want to be.

Now, when the mission, values, and beliefs of an organization honors who I am as a person, magic happens! To see and hear myself reflected in both the staff and learners in our community is an incredibly empowering experience. To be able to model for young ones and for families is also very gratifying. For the first time, my personal self is allowed to shine and come through. Authentic engagement and collaboration can take place. It is much less taxing on my personal energy stores; not having to think about who to be and how to engage in a way that makes others feel "okay" is life changing.

For the first time, I've been able to experience belonging at work, which to me means showing up authentically without fear or worry about being "too" anything. Not needing to be thinking about code-switching or living only part of your truth. Feeling safe and secure—to express thoughts, feelings, emotions, and behaviors aligned to your authentic true self. Seeing and feeling heard and understood. Seeing others who are like you. Having an organization that values one another and helps others to see and understand the differences and similarities that we have. Proactively engaging in discourse and learning around belonging, equity, and inclusivity—structures that exist and are in place to expose microaggressions and situations that impact other people's sense of belonging.

My advice to organizations looking to create this sense of belonging in their workplaces? Own your stuff and know your blind spots . . . and if you can't do that, hire someone who can help!

THE NEED TO BELONG

In a 1995 study, Baumeister and Leary showed that human beings are "fundamentally and pervasively motivated by a need to belong" and to "form and maintain enduring interpersonal attachments."[6] They concluded their study by stating that psychology has underappreciated the importance of the need to belong, and stated that the "desire for interpersonal attachment may well be one of the most far-reaching and integrative constructs currently available to understand human nature."

The need to belong, it would seem, transcends cultures, geographies, genders, and generations. It represents a primal, or basic, human instinct.

Humans are relational beings. So strong is our need to belong that we will endure extremely trying—even harmful—circumstances to belong. Baby mammals, including humans, will repeatedly return to their primary caregiver (or attachment figure, as we will define it in an upcoming section) even if that primary caregiver is biting, kicking, or punching them. We bend ourselves out of shape trying to fit in, attempting to

---

[6] Baumeister and Leary, "The Need to Belong: Desire for Interpersonal Attachments as a Fundamental Human Motivation," 497–529.

become a different size puzzle piece so we can force ourselves into the overall jigsaw puzzle and create that picture on the front of the box. (Remember high school?)

That effort to be something or someone you are not comes at a psychological cost. It is hard work to dumb down, repress, suppress, or switch off parts of your personality, behavior, or identity to be deemed acceptable enough to receive nurture and love and experience belonging with other people. Doing so requires a significant amount of mental and emotional energy. In the world of work specifically, if somebody feels threatened or that they can't be themselves, they will bend themselves out of shape to fit in—and in so doing, they will divert that psychological energy toward the process of changing or covering themselves.

Of course (as we saw in the Introduction), if they don't have to do that—if they feel a sense of belonging and safety in the workplace—all the energy that is otherwise occupied maintaining a false self can be released and channeled into the work. Doing a better job is a result of showing up authentically—but showing up authentically can only happen if there's no psychological cost to it. It happens when I think my authentic self is going to be accepted, loved, nurtured, and cared for and I am made to feel like I belong. And when I do show up authentically, all of me is available for work—for performing my job—as opposed to only 50 percent being available because the other 50 percent is worried about who to be or not be to be deemed acceptable.

In this chapter, we will look at the psychology of belonging through the lenses of Self psychology, Attachment Theory, and trauma-informed workplaces.

SELF PSYCHOLOGY

I'd like to start this exploration of the psychology of belonging with a brief tour of Self psychology, the work of psychoanalyst Heinz Kohut.

In the sixties, Kohut explored narcissism in new ways,[7] ultimately leading to the development of his deeply influential body of work, Self psychology. The core tenets of this body of work that have the most resonance with the topic of belonging include the Self, selfobjects, and selfobject experiences of mirroring, idealizing, twinship, and empathy, each of which plays a crucial role in the healthy development of humans. Self psychology provides us with a model for understanding how we develop our own internal sense of Self, with the idea that the

---

[7] Narcissism does not necessarily represent a surplus of self-esteem, but more accurately, it encompasses a hunger for appreciation or admiration, a desire to be the center of attention, and an expectation of special treatment.

more robust our self-concept, the more we feel like we belong. Stated simply, Self psychology is a way of understanding how we become ourselves in relation to other people.

Some of these core tenets of Self psychology also go on to have lifelong importance for the maintenance of healthy self-esteem in adults and the belonging they can, and do, experience in the workplace. Self psychology isn't directly about how to belong; it's about knowing who we are and how we have developed into who we are—the ingredients that are important for developing that sense of Self. Being at home in oneself, and being able to belong to oneself, is an important part of feeling belonging with others. Self psychology is a way of strengthening and developing the idea of who you are as a person, and of being able to recognize the ways in which people can build their self-esteem and encourage them to step more into their identity and their self-concept. Leaders need to understand these tenets of Self psychology, both to become more authentically themselves and experience belonging, and also to create the spaces where other people feel safe to be *their* most authentic selves, bringing all of who they are to the workplace instead of spending energy covering who they really are.

Here I will briefly explain each core concept and demonstrate its pertinence to facilitating the experience of belonging in the workplace.

THE SELF

Kohut was a psychoanalyst, and unlike some other psycho-analytic theorists, he viewed the Self as having its own line of development that should ideally lead to a creative, loving, and cohesive whole person. The development of the Self, he said, happens in relationship with other people and in response to certain fundamental needs being met through selfobject experiences of mirroring, idealization, and twinship (concepts that will be discussed in more detail in later sections of this chapter).

Relationships are fundamental to the successful operation of any business and workplace. Even "individual contributors" are not an island and must work with others to achieve goals and deliver results.[8] We have all had the experience, I am sure, of working alongside people who are not bringing their full Self to their work and for whom we have picked up the slack in some way. It gets tiring very quickly, doesn't it?

Imagine, for a moment, what it would do to performance, morale, and company culture if every person you'll ever work alongside felt willing and able to bring their whole Self to work. To that end, the idea of companies needing to develop

---

[8] Individual contributors: A term used in corporations to describe specialists who occupy roles without direct reports or team members.

whole, cohesive, creative, and caring employees couldn't be more apropos.

SELFOBJECTS

Kohut defined selfobjects as an inner depiction of an external object.[9] In other words, as part of our development, we experience, learn from, and then internalize aspects of people and experiences around us and incorporate them into our own sense of Self as though they are part of ourselves. Thus, it is crucial for a child to have functional and positive interactions with their selfobjects to establish a firm and healthy sense of well-being. For example, the infant child can internalize, as a selfobject, a primary caregiver's love and nurture in such a way that the primary caregiver does not need to be physically present for the child to have the experience of said love and nurture.

Selfobjects are acquired through "selfobject experiences." As we mature, humans tend to experience certain contexts in which selfobject experiences impact our development and growth, starting as an infant in our home life and our family of origin (however that is defined by the individual), then into

---

[9] Inspired by Klein's 1998 theory of the unconscious, Object Relations Theory, the word "object" is used in contrast to "subject" and in relation to a person, experience, or thing that is outside of the Self but that comes to be recognized and experienced as being part of the Self.

childhood and adolescence in school, then into the professional context during adulthood. At each stage of development, and in every context, it is necessary for the person to have healthy and constructive mirroring, idealizing, and twinship selfobject experiences to maintain a cohesive sense of Self and well-being. Ergo, while a child's first selfobject experiences come from their primary caregiver(s), the need for healthy selfobject experiences continues throughout the lifespan.

Noting that this includes the professional context, let's move on to discuss the three types of selfobject experiences and how they might manifest in the world of work.

Mirroring

The fundamental need met by a mirroring selfobject is having one's "sense of vigor, greatness, and perfection" confirmed—or mirrored back—by other people.[10] This highlights the importance of primary caregivers, teachers, siblings, and other family members providing affirmation to the young child to help them develop a cohesive sense of Self.

As an adult, and in the world of work in particular, mirroring selfobject experiences might come in the form of reassuring

---

[10] Mitchell and Black, *Freud and Beyond: A History of Modern Psychoanalytic Thought*.

colleagues, formal and informal recognition of your work, or perhaps a promotion.

Can you imagine how you would feel at work if your own vigor, greatness, or perfection was not mirrored back to you at all? What would happen to your performance? Your discretionary effort? Your concentration and commitment? Your attendance/absence levels?

Additionally, if you work in a place where there is an absence of other people who look like you—an absence of diversity—then you are not mirrored. You don't have other people to look up to. It doesn't take too much of a stretch to see the importance of mirroring selfobject experiences to the concept of belonging in the workplace.

Idealizing

The fundamental need met by an idealizing selfobject is having others who the child can look up to and who they can merge with "as an image of calmness, infallibility, and omnipotence."[11] In short, a child needs positive role models they can aspire to be like and take inspiration from to develop a cohesive sense of Self.

---

[11] Kohut and Wolf, "The Disorders of the Self and their Treatment: An Outline," 413–425.

For me, the idealizing selfobject experience underlines the important role that managers and leaders play in terms of enabling people to feel as though they belong. Over the past two decades, I have taught leadership development classes and coached executives around the principle, "leadership is a behavior, not a title," which encourages them to reflect on the fact that their leadership is not defined by their pay grade but through the extent to which they have followers.[12]

The primary question asked when I share this principle with leaders is, "Well, how do I get/keep followers?" My answer is an amalgam of thinking from thought leaders such as Robert Goffee and Gareth Jones, Daniel Goleman, the late Stephen R. Covey, and Simon Sinek, which is to guide them to bring their full Selves to their leadership role—that is, with increasing amounts of skill and behavioral flexibility.[13] When leaders demonstrate this behavior, they give permission and pave the way for others to do so through an idealizing self-object experience.

---

[12] Seems a bit too obvious to say this, but leadership can only exist if there is followership.

[13] The right to be your full Self comes with some responsibilities in terms of personal accountability for ethical, moral, legal, and collaborative behavior.

Why is this important? Well, remember how I shared the experience I, and likely you, had at high school, of needing to hide, diminish, or cover up parts of myself to be accepted and feel like I belonged? An aspect of our experience of belonging is inextricably linked to the extent to which we can be our full Self and be accepted for doing so. Leaders who role model that it is okay to be your full Self (yes, with increasing amounts of skill and behavioral flexibility) will create teams and workplaces that role model this concept.

Twinship

The fundamental need met by a twinship selfobject experience is having peers who, in their openness and similarity, evoke a sense of likeness between the child and themselves.

This is the simplest and easiest selfobject experience to associate to the concept of belonging in the workplace. When workers look up, down, and to the side, do they see their likeness in their coworkers? Do they see Black, Brown, and mixed-race colleagues, or are they lost in a sea of whiteness? Does a female-identified person see someone she can identify with in the executive team, or are they all occupying junior positions? Can a member of LGBTQIA2+ community talk openly with people like them about the challenges they face in a heteronormative world, or do they have to "cover"?[14] Does a person who is blind experience aloneness because people overlook their needs? How about the person who is neurodiverse —do they experience twinship?

The mirroring, idealizing, and twinship aspects of Self psychology are important to maintaining and boosting one's self-esteem. To be yourself, you've got to know who you are *and* you need external affirmation from the people around you, letting you know that who you are is okay.

EMPATHY

Kohut viewed empathy as "the capacity to think and feel oneself into the inner life of another person,"[15] and he believed it to be as fundamental to the building blocks of human experience as the five senses and as important to successful human development as oxygen is to human life. Central to Kohut's theory is the understanding that the Self can best be understood through empathy rather than through insight.

---

[14] Cover: The behavior of hiding or muting the expression or visibility of some aspect of one's identity (parts of the Self) based on the belief that this characteristic may cause one to be stigmatized, marginalized, or excluded by others.

[15] Kohut, *The Analysis of the Self: A Systematic Approach to the Psychoanalytic Treatment of Narcissistic Personality Disorder*.

Empathy and sympathy are not synonymous; understanding the subtle but important difference is crucial in the context of facilitating the experience of belonging. I like to think of sympathy as "feeling *for*" and empathy as "feeling *with*" another person. Dr. Brené Brown, a researcher, author, public speaker, and social worker from Texas explains that "empathy drives connection while sympathy drives disconnection."[16] She also says that empathy involves:

- Taking perspective: Recognizing someone else's experience as valid and as being their map of the world.

- Staying out of judgment: Avoiding the temptation to evaluate, assess, or reframe someone else's truth.

- Recognizing emotion in other people and being able to communicate that: Being able to name feelings that other people are having and being able to let them know that you can name them.

The topic of empathy (and perhaps more famously, vulnerability) was thrust into the limelight of the professional world in 2010 through Brené Brown's TED Talk, "The Power of

---

[16] RSA, "Brené Brown on Empathy," https://www.youtube.com/watch?v=1Evwgu369 Jw&t=2s.

Vulnerability." Since its release, it has become one of the most-watched TED Talks of all time (with more than fifty million views at the time of writing this book), and Brown's vast body of work has become a key source of inspiration and conversation in my leadership development, executive coaching, and clinical work.

It's not just Brown who argues for the importance of empathy in the workplace. Dozens of authors have spoken to this topic, including well-known people such as Daniel Goleman, Simon Sinek, and Oprah Winfrey. But it is Dr. Jayson Boyers, the president of Rosemont College, who put it best for me when he said:

> One of the hallmarks of a successful business is its ability to harness creativity to constantly push into new territory. Without growth and innovation, businesses stagnate and eventually fade away. Those with staying power, however, have mastered an intangible, often overlooked factor that allows them to focus on the future with clarity: empathy. While that may surprise many, I am certain that the ability to connect with and relate to others—empathy in its purest form—is the force that moves businesses forward.[17]

---

[17] Boyers, "Why Empathy Is the Force That Moves Business Forward."

With this clarity as to what empathy is, it is also important to understand that empathy is a developable skill; it is something we can all learn to do—and do better.

There are four components to empathy:

1. The ability to assume positive intent

2. The ability to give people the benefit of the doubt

3. The ability to meet people where they are at

4. The ability to listen with the intent to understand

Let's take a closer look at each.

Assume Positive Intent

Assuming positive intent is not the same as letting people walk all over you or letting them off the hook—and it certainly doesn't mean *not* holding other people accountable for their behavior. Instead, assuming positive intent is an active, conscious process of recognizing and remembering that we are all doing the best we can with the resources we have available to us. None of us get up in the morning to come to work and deliberately do a bad a job. When we encounter roadblocks, when we stumble, when things go wrong or we make mistakes, or when people make us mad or tread on our toes—when we lead with empathy and assume a positive intent, we can approach these situations from a place of, "This person didn't deliberately set out to mess up. We're all human, and mistakes happen for everyone. They're likely trying their hardest too."

Give People the Benefit of the Doubt

Giving people the benefit of the doubt is a well-recognized idea of suppressing our suspicions about other people unless and until proven otherwise. In so doing, we are demonstrating that we respect their model of the world. Giving the benefit of the doubt is a posture of softening. We can then show up as someone who is interested, curious, and open. This allows you to use the constructive side of doubt, instead of the negative side. The result? Solving problems from a place of giving the benefit of the doubt is infinitely easier and more enjoyable for everyone involved.

Meet People Where They Are At

It is far easier to go to somebody else's bus stop and ask them to get on your bus than it is for you to convince them to walk to your bus stop and then also ride your bus. Meeting people where they're at means that rather than trying to convince someone that your way is the right way, you take a moment or two to explore, unpack, and respect where they are coming from and the many ways in which they interpret the world. This concept can show up in various forms. For example, coaching team members to arrive at their own answers, managing people toward outcomes, or allowing them to speak and share their perspectives before you give yours. You will quickly see a shift in people's performance when you meet them where they're at instead of having them meet you where you are.

Listen With the Intent to Understand

Stephen R. Covey, author of *The 7 Habits of Highly Effective People*, says that most people don't listen with the intent to understand; they listen with the intent to reply. Someone who is listening only with the intent to reply is not actually listening. They are waiting to talk, queuing up words in their head, perhaps formulating a clever retort or smart question to react to a portion of what someone else has said. When you listen with the intent to understand, however, you take in everything the person has said and respond directly to it.

It doesn't take a genius to work out that building up empathy is a good thing. When you lead with empathy, people are likely to feel safer admitting that they don't know an answer, apologizing, asking for help, or admitting mistakes. When empathy is present, the fear around saying those vulnerable things is ameliorated or even eliminated. (And in Chapter 2, we'll see just why it's so important that people be able to express these thoughts.)

ATTACHMENT THEORY

No conversation about the psychology of belonging can be complete without an exploration of John Bowlby's Attachment Theory, which centralizes the importance of forming affectional bonds and the consequences of losing them, including disruption to the healthy development and ongoing psychological health of human beings. Bowlby establishes early on into the explication of his theory the importance of social groups and goes onto say that "human infants, we can safely conclude, like infants in other species, are preprogrammed to develop in a socially cooperative way; whether they do so or not turns in high degree on how they are treated."[18]

In this, he clearly articulates that humans need each other and confirms that the manner in which we develop depends on how we treat each other. In short, no person is an island and no person can rely simply on themselves for healthy

---

[18] Bowlby, *A Secure Base: Parent–Child Attachment and Healthy Human Development.*

development; the need for interaction with others and the need to belong are baked into our psyche.

Bowlby sets out some key concepts within Attachment Theory that I believe are pertinent to our exploration of belonging in the workplace:

- **Attachment figure:** A target for proximity-seeking which functions as a safe haven in times of need, serves as a "secure base" in a safe environment, and whose real or expected disappearance induces "separation distress." A bit like healthy selfobject experiences, attachment figures might show up in the world of work in the guise of an approachable boss, a best work friend, a mentor, or a trusted colleague.

- **Secure base:** An environment provided through a relationship with one or more sensitive and responsive attachment figures who meet the child's needs and provide safe haven for the child when upset or anxious. A secure base is akin to Donald Winnicott's "holding environment," which he described as the creation of a supportive, nurturing environment that results in a sense of trust and safety.[19] Secure

---

[19] Rodman, *Winnicott: His Life and Work*.

bases at work might show up in the form of a team in which you feel appreciated, understood, cared for, and enabled. I've lost count of the times I have seen "team environment" show up in exit interviews and employee opinion surveys as a reason for low morale and high attrition. When we don't have a secure base, we will go to extraordinary lengths to find one, and yes, sometimes that means leaving a salaried job without another one to go to. On the surface, rationally, that might seem reckless, but when it comes to belonging, we're talking neither "surface" nor "rational;" we're in the space of deep, primal, unconscious needs for affection, nurture, and care.

- **Separation anxiety:** The experience of severe discomfort to actual or potential unwelcome separations from or losses of an attachment figure. What might cause separation anxiety at work? Trusted colleagues leaving, new bosses arriving, reallocations to new departments, desk moves, and restructures all fall into the category of potential sources of separation anxiety.

Although Bowlby was primarily focused on understanding the nature of the infant–caregiver relationship, he believed that attachment characterized human experience from the cradle to the grave. According to R. Chris Fraley, a professor of psychology at the University of Illinois at Urbana-Champaign, it was not until the mid-eighties, however, that researchers began to take seriously the possibility that attachment processes may play out in adulthood. Fraley says that research on adult attachment is guided by the assumption that the same motivational system that gives rise to the close emotional bond between parents and their children is responsible for the bond that develops adult-to-adult.[20]

PSYCHOLOGICAL SAFETY

While seminal, Bowlby's work wasn't the first talk about the importance of belonging. Beyond Freud's assertion in 1930 that we are "never so helplessly unhappy as when we have lost our loved object or its love,"[21] it is probably A. H. Maslow who is best known for introducing the topic of belonging to psychological discourse when he ranked "love and belongingness needs" in the middle of his motivational hierarchy of needs.[22]

While the term "psychological safety" wouldn't be coined until 1965 by Schein and Bennis,[23] and then applied to the workplace

---

[20] Fraley, "Adult Attachment Theory and Research: A Brief Overview."

[21] Freud, *Civilization and its Discontents.*

[22] Maslow, "A Theory of Human Motivation."

[23] Bennis, *Organization Development: Its Nature, Origins, and Prospects.*

in 1990 by William Kahn,[24] it is clear that Maslow, Schein and Bennis, and Kahn were all talking about the same thing: certain physiological safety needs (e.g., food and shelter) must be taken care of before psychological safety needs become a priority.

Clark concurs with Maslow, Schein and Bennis, and Kahn, and at the same time resonates with the definition of belonging offered above when he says, "Psychological safety is a condition in which you feel included, safe to learn, safe to contribute, and safe to challenge the status quo—all without fear of being embarrassed, marginalized, or punished in some way."[25]

Clark also describes how the presence of four different types of psychological safety (inclusion safety, learner safety, contributor safety, and challenger safety, each described in more detail momentarily) enable employees to bring their full Self to work, and that when they can bring their full Self to work, they, the teams to which they belong, and the organizations of which they are a part, will flourish. He predicts that in the twenty-first century, high psychological safety will increasingly become a term of employment, and organizations that don't supply it will "bleed out their top talent."

---

[24] Kahn, "Psychological Conditions of Personal Engagement and Disengagement at Work."

[25] Clark, *The 4 Stages of Psychological Safety: Defining the Path to Inclusion and Innovation*.

Inclusion Safety

Inclusion safety is the first stage of psychological safety. It occurs when an outsider to a team is accepted as an insider, is welcomed to be part of that team, and gains a shared identity.

I experienced a lack of inclusion safety in high school, which resonates with Clark's position when he says that this type of inclusion is "not an attempt to cover up differences or politely pretend they are not there," but is, in fact, a process of genuinely inviting another to no longer be an "other," "based on the sole qualification that they possess flesh and blood."[26]

Learner Safety

The presence of learner safety, the next stage of psychological safety, is crucial in organizational teams because without it, Clark asserts, individuals will not ask questions, they will not experiment and innovate, and they will not feel safe in making—and learning from—mistakes. Learner safety can occur when the individual is not being belittled, demeaned, or harshly corrected by the team leader and their fellow team members.

---

[26] Clark, *The 4 Stages of Psychological Safety*.

Contributor Safety

Clark's third stage of psychological safety is contributor safety, which enables the individual to participate as a full-fledged member of the team. Clark says that contributor safety emerges when the individual performs well in the delivery of their accountabilities, receives encouragement from fellow team members, is granted autonomy, and sees a demonstration of the team leader's belief in them. (I will talk more about the crucial role of the team leader in the development of inclusive workplaces in an upcoming section and in later chapters.)

Challenger Safety

The final stage of psychological safety, challenger safety, occurs when the individual is granted high levels of respect and permission by members of the team and the team's leader. This level of psychological safety enables the individual to "challenge the status quo without retribution, reprisal, or the risk of damaging (their) personal standing or reputation."[27]

---

[27] Clark, *The 4 Stages of Psychological Safety*.

TRAUMA-INFORMED
WORKPLACES

I would now like to consider the concept of psychological safety in the workplace from a trauma-informed angle.

As previously mentioned, the way this decade (the 2020s) started has been like no other. With the COVID-19 pandemic leading many companies like Google, Twitter, and Apple to enforce indefinite working from home conditions; increases in social uprising; an American presidential race that caught the attention of the world; and the Oxford English Dictionary's choice to expand its word of the year (in 2020) to encompass several words of an "unprecedented year" with entries such as bushfires, COVID-19, WFH, lockdown, circuit-breaker, support bubbles, keyworkers, furlough, Black Lives Matter, and moonshot.

While I, along with many others, including the American Psychological Association, contemplate the long-term psychological impacts of 2020, from a personal perspective, I don't think I have ever received, nor sent, so many emails that started with the phrase, "I hope you are well in these strange and unprecedented times." Nor have I ever finished more emails with the phrase, "Be well," and considered the depth, meaning, and poignancy of those words and how they were intended to land for the recipient in the context of a pervasively violent and chronically harmful year. Whether or not folks have overtly stated this (to themselves or to others), our concept of psychological safety has been threatened, shaken, and placed in a constant state of jeopardy for an extended period throughout the majority of 2020 and into 2021.

Safety is a subjective experience; the interpersonal and intrapersonal extent to which we feel safe differs and changes through time contextually. Dr Ziggy Frome, a character in NBC's hit show *New Amsterdam* said it best: "Trauma doesn't happen because you're in danger; it's because you *think* you are."[28] Although these are the words of a fictional character, they resonate deeply as being true, as evidenced in my clinical work with clients who have experienced complex trauma and who meet the criteria for a diagnosis of post-traumatic stress disorder (PTSD).

Companies around the world this year have been setting up "safe spaces" or "safe rooms" for employees to discuss and process the impact the events of the early 2020s have had, and continue to have, on them. While the creation of these spaces is undoubtedly well-intended and has, unquestionably, gone

---

[28] *New Amsterdam*, season 2, episode 16, "Perspectives."

a long way in reducing the harm done by an *annus horribilis*,[29] I am mindful that what represents safety for some may not feel safe for others, and that we have no real way of telling, predicting, or ensuring conditions of safety. I also have in mind a series of harm-reduction conversations I have been involved in through my clinical work at Pacific Center for Human Growth,[30] in which we have explored the concept of safe spaces and how, oftentimes, the person claiming a space to be safe will be someone with identity markers from the dominant group and will do so from a place of privilege.[31]

Again, these people are likely well-intended, but as a trusted colleague reminded me, people with identity markers from the subordinate group are never going to be fully safe in a space held by someone with identity markers from the dominant group. (We will discuss what workplaces can do instead, creating and facilitating "intentionally brave spaces," in a later chapter.)

---

[29] *Annus horribilis* is a Latin phrase, meaning "horrible year."

[30] Pacific Center for Human Growth in Berkley, California is one of the USA's oldest LGBTQIA2+ clinics. The clinic centers mental health as a social justice issue and provides much needed counseling services to people living in the margins of society.

[31] Dominant group identity markers include people who are white, male-bodied, cisgender, heterosexual, or able-bodied, whereas subordinate group identity markers include people who are *not* white, male-bodied, cisgender, heterosexual, or able-bodied.

A STORY OF BELONGING

PK is a Black, heteroflexible, cisgender female in her early thirties who lives and works in Manhattan, New York.

IF YOU ASK ME TO DEFINE BELONGING, I WOULD BREAK IT into two parts, although I recognize that there are a number of factors that influence these pillars:

1. Fundamental inclusion: My ability to see reflections of my unique experience in the workplace and that those experiences be respected across the organization.

2. Long-term growth: My access to upward mobility within that organization.

Of the four organizations I've worked in in the advertising industry, I've not had a workplace that offered both fundamental inclusion and long-term growth in satisfying doses. However, as a Black woman, it has never been my expectation that I would be in a workplace where belonging was something I could even consider. I've been conditioned to temper my expectations, and so when workplaces offer even shades of those two core tenets of belonging, I just accept the offer and don't challenge for more.

With these lowered expectations, there are two examples where I experienced a degree of belonging.

The first was at a smaller, independently run media services agency. Here, I was given great opportunities for mobility. I felt like my contributions were valued and recognized with lateral and vertical movements that allowed me to grow my expertise. I also saw versions of myself represented in senior leadership (albeit sparsely). When in this space where I was confident my work would be rewarded, it helped me feel more inclined to produce good work.

My second experience with belonging is with my most recent media agency, which exists as one of many brands under a larger holding company. Here, I have been given autonomy and support to create spaces where unique experiences can be valued. This gives me the opportunity to build new skills and grow in ways that fall outside of the original scope of the job.

Although I share these examples where I have felt some sense of belonging, I have noticed a disturbing trend within the industry: there are very few people of color in leadership positions, and those that do exist are not always as visible or as accessible as they could be to make an impact on those looking up to them. This also places an undue burden on those few to have to be representatives, which can contribute to the reason they leave the industry.

It can seem like wasted energy to invest in an organization that has shown it won't invest in you in the same ways. It became difficult for me to see a future in the industry, which can translate into not seeing the value of meeting the potential of my performance.

I believe companies should consider long-term growth as a major part of belonging. If I can't see myself in the future of the organization, did I really ever belong at all?

As this chapter ends, I would like to offer the following conclusions:

- **Belonging is a human need.** It is clear that the need to belong is a fundamental part of the human developmental experience, which extends into adulthood. It is also clear that the presence of psychological safety is a prerequisite for a sense of belonging. When people experience psychological safety *and* a sense of belonging, they feel more able to be fully themselves.

- **Belonging is relational.** The quality of the relationship that someone has with themselves and the quality of the relationship someone has with others impacts the extent to which they will experience belonging.

- **Empathy is necessary for belonging to occur.** If empathy is "feeling with" other people, there must be other people—in quality relationships—with whom to feel.

With increased clarity as to the psychological nature of belonging, I'd like to address the question I'm sure is on your mind: *why is it necessary to create the experience of belonging in the workplace?* Chapter 2 shows you how a culture of belonging is good for business.

A CULTURE OF BELONGING IS GOOD FOR BUSINESS

"With our arms interlocked,
the sun shone on us a feeling of safety and
respect, a deep sense of belonging."

—Ian Mitchell, Psy.D., Head of Performance Psychology
for the UK Football Association, after the team
made it to the finals of the Euro Cup

W B is a white, bisexual, cisgender woman in her late thirties who lives and works in London, England.

FOR ME, BELONGING IN THE WORKPLACE SIGNIFIES
that I can be myself; I don't have to hide myself, and I still
feel like I belong to my team and my company. I feel connected to the people I work with, and they are important to
me. It means I can feel comfortable sharing about my private
life and my background.

Feeling like I belong makes me work harder, as I want to
do right by my team and make sure that they get the best
of me. I think it also helps motivate me to do a good job, and
I feel content to work and progress at a company where
I feel safe and happy (so I am not actively looking for a
different job).

I am fortunate in that I have not worked for a company
where I did not feel I belonged. This ad agency has been my
home for over eight years now. The people I get to work
with, under the conditions set by the workplace, and the
projects I get to work on mean that I feel like I belong, and I
am loyal to this employer. The international environment

and clients I get to work with also suit my varied interests and have allowed me to use my native and learned languages, which made me feel like I could live out multiple parts within me.

I also feel like I can be fully myself without having to pretend to be someone I'm not. I feel accepted and liked by the people around me, and while they are all different, they are tolerant of others and allow me to share my true self without having to fear rejection.

Because I can be myself, I feel like I don't need to waste energy pretending to be someone I'm not—energy I am then able to put back into my work, to make sure my team does well and our clients are happy. I go the extra mile—taking that client call on a Friday evening, even though I could have just turned my phone off for the weekend—and I also want to share knowledge I have gained, as I want the company to succeed.

CULTURE ON THE FRONTLINES

Somewhere between Peter Drucker's assertion that "Culture eats strategy for breakfast," Netflix's famous culture deck, and the rise of staff canteens so good that the public wants to pay to eat at them, culture has become a hot commodity in the war for talent.

There have been several waves in the commoditization of culture:

- **The need for freedom.** The first wave included the welcome demise of the "dress code" (I mean, really, who on earth measures the hem length of their dress?), the move to open-plan office seating and the gradual dissolution of glass offices (noise-canceling headphones anyone?), and the introduction of increasing amounts of flexible working policies (I want to earn a salary and live my life, thank you very much. Hand me the cake because I am going to eat that too!).

- **The need for connection.** The entrance of Gen Y into the workforce heralded the next cultural wave. Here is a group of people who favor outcomes over process and emotional and mental presence over physical output. This is also a community who wants to connect their purpose to the organization's, feel good while they do good, and invest their care in an organization that cares for them in return. Organizations that got good at being mission-driven and values-centric, and that went all-in on philanthropic causes, started to win. So did the companies that offered the best pantry snacks and self-filling candy jars. Long gone were the days of being grateful for on-tap filter coffee and a choice of two teabags!

- **The need for belonging.** But fancy cold brew, artisanal dried pineapple, and micro-brewed IPA soon became table stakes in a world where one's identity is at risk and where being yourself can be problematic. As the world began to respond with increasing visibility to issues of racism, sexism, homophobia, and transphobia, a new need arose and with it a new cultural wave: a need to belong.

As we have already established, the need for belonging is within all of us. For organizations to become successful and stay successful, they need to invest in creating a culture of belonging—one where people feel as though they can be themselves so that they are freed up to do great work.

Let's look at this concept of a culture of belonging through three separate but related lenses: the individual lens, the team lens, and the organization lens.

THE INDIVIDUAL LENS

In an article entitled, "I'm a Straight White Guy—What's Diversity Got to Do With Me?", Walt Hopkins writes, "Diversity begins with me. I need to understand myself before I can understand you."[32] It is from this quote that I take inspiration for this individual lens of the culture of belonging.

Over the course of my career, I've had the honor of running hundreds of workshops and learning experiences with groups of people on every single continent around the globe. These workshops have gone beyond unconscious bias and explore the topics of identity and privilege.[33] Time and again, group members have found strength in recognizing that, whoever they are, different aspects of their identity can in some way or another carry privilege. They have come to realize that instead of being ashamed of that privilege, they can own it and use it to support, elevate, and advocate for those people who could

---

[32] Hopkins, "I'm a Straight White Guy—So What's Diversity Got to Do With Me?"

[33] See *Privilege: A Reader* by Michael S. Kimmel and Abby L. Ferber for a solid exploration of what is meant by privilege and how it shows up in society.

otherwise be marginalized, oppressed, or "othered" because they are different.

Once you know yourself more, then comes the job of knowing others. Here I counsel some caution: it is not the job of people who are different from us to educate us about their struggles and experiences…that's on us. It is crucial that we find ways to grow our own awareness and wake up to the experiences of people not like us. (There are tons of resources out there; my recommendations can be found in the Appendix.)

I got a top tip from a good friend of mine recently: she asked me who I followed on Instagram and how many of those people I followed were like me and how many were dissimilar to me. It's surprising how many messages of reinforcement and conditioning we can receive through Instagram! In asking this very simple question, my friend opened my eyes to the extent to which I was reinforcing my own worldview and restricting my awareness to difference and diversity. Now my Instagram feed[34] is no longer just my favorite waste of time; it is also an important source of education.

---

[34] https://www.instagram.com/soul_trained

THE TEAM LENS

In the eighties, Dr. Meredith Belbin famously pronounced that, "Nobody is perfect, but a team can be." While significant at the time, today this seems a bit "Thanks, Captain Obvious," doesn't it?

But let's take a moment or two to consider a leader's unconscious biases, which might cause them to build a team in their own likeness. It can be very tempting, if we are not careful, to surround ourselves with like-minded others—those with similar skills, backgrounds, and experiences to us. After all, it feels safe, warm, and comforting to be with "people like us."

I was working recently with a leader who told me they wanted to be the least skilled person on their team. They wanted to be the person who knew less than anyone else and who had less of an idea about what to do and where to head than anyone else. I was in awe of the ease at which they explored an experience of not-knowingness; it seemed to me that they had let go of something in order to make space for something greater.

It has been shown time and again that teams of diverse individuals are smarter than homogenous teams.[35] And we're not

---

[35] Roth and Grant, "Why Diverse Teams Are Smarter."

just talking about diversity in skills or experience; we're talking about diversity in sex, gender, ethnicity, race, ability, sexuality, socioeconomic background, age, religion and so on. Difference is strength, and an acceptance of difference opens the avenues toward belonging and inclusion.

THE ORGANIZATION LENS

"Cultural fabric" is the collective noun I use to describe the wiring that powers organizational culture. In short, a cultural fabric is the vision, mission, values, behaviors, motifs, customs, and rituals that comprise an organization's culture. Cultural fabrics remain as relevant in today's organization as they were in the fifties when Peter Drucker first started talking about the topic. Values systems act as the moral compass of a company, and behavioral frameworks become the means by which these values are expressed and brought to bear in the day-to-day interactions of employees.

Relationships and the way people treat each other are the wellspring of any culture. Because of this, our behaviors—how we interact with each other as we do our work, how we talk to each other, what we say about other people when they are not in the room, and particularly how we treat each other in times of stress, conflict, and overwhelm—impact culture in deeply profound and systemic ways.

To that end, a company that wants to foster a culture of belonging could take the first step by reviewing what's included in their values systems. Of course, the perennial favorites of "teamwork, collaboration, and personal responsibility" (or less corporate-ese versions thereof) remain important when groups of people come together, but perhaps they are no longer enough.

I'm suggesting that now is the time for organizations to make a brave statement about what's important and what's not by evolving the ingredients of their cultural fabrics to include different qualities—vulnerability, courage, patience, curiosity, empathy, and acceptance, to name just a few.

THE EXPERIENCE
OF BELONGING AT WORK

A ton of research exists that explores and explains how important and highly-correlated employee happiness is with performance, but there seems to be a dearth of peer-reviewed articles on the impact of being able to be oneself or how the experience of being oneself at work correlates to performance.

In 2008, two researchers, McClure and Brown, conducted a phenomenological study which explored the concept of belonging at work by asking, "What is the experience of belonging at work?" The researchers collected verbal data from twelve respondents of a range of ages who worked in public and private sector companies, and they concluded that further research into the impact of belonging on employee effectiveness is called for. They concluded that, "people needed help learning how to be at work and that they continued to learn and develop different ways of relating to other employees and to their work. It is a story of growing self in relation to others while involved in productive enterprise." Adding credence to the need for this book, they went on to say that "it would be interesting to explore further...the costs to the enterprise of employees feeling like they do not belong," and called for further research that would establish an "optimum level of belonging."[36]

Clinical psychologist Amanda Kottler linked the experience of belonging to the need for twinship as described in Kohut's Self psychology (as you read about in Chapter 1). She describes how the state of belonging is cultivated by twinship self-object experiences and how the absence of such experiences can lead to alienation—in other words, the experience of *not* belonging. She states, "It is from a place of belonging and feeling at home that we can relax and 'be' human among other human

---

[36] McClure and Brown, "Belonging at Work."

beings, who can in turn, 'be' themselves," and in doing so draw an important link between the experience of belonging and feeling as though you can be yourself. In her conclusion, Kottler also talks about the importance of people "being at home in themselves."[37]

This has exciting implications for the concept of belonging in the workplace because, thus far, my exploration of the literature had left me with the impression that the experience of belonging lay entirely in the hands of other people. With Kottler's words, we can entertain the thought that the experience of belonging is actually a two-sided coin: on one side, we have the action or inaction of other people dictating the experience of belonging, and on the other side, we see that an individual has agency in their experience of belonging.

Building on this, four methodologically diverse studies explored the link between belonging and meaning and concluded that "relationships that promote a sense of belonging are especially likely to promote a belief that one's life is meaningful."[38] While this does give rise to additional questions—such as, "What aspects of someone's experience at work lead

---

[37] Kottler, "Feeling at Home, Belonging, and Being Human: Kohut, Self Psychology, Twinship, and Alienation."

[38] Lambert et al., "To Belong is to Matter: Sense of Belonging Enhances Meaning in Life."

them to feel like they belong?" and "Does a sense of meaning in life lead to greater performance within the workplace?"—it also makes the case for a sense of belonging being an important aspect of one's sense of meaning.

If we can accept that one can have a relationship with one's work, I believe that Lambert et al., in their conclusion, were able to draw important links between a workplace in which one feels as though they belong and the experience of meaning in life and, therefore, overall well-being and increased ability to perform and deliver workplace objectives and goals.

Simon Sinek agrees with this perspective and states that employees and organizations that have a strong "why" will perform better than those who do not. Wrzensiewski, on the other hand, states that the benefits of an organization ensuring its employees experience meaning in their work look "promising" in relation to the organization's performance.[39]

I would go further in combining the view of Sinek and Wrzensiewski with my own experience and the experiences of hundreds of people I have worked with, interviewed, and coached over the last two decades to say that we perform better and are able to give more when we're not worried about

---

[39] Wrzesniewski, "Finding Positive Meaning in Work," 296–308.

whether we belong amongst the people we think of as our colleagues and peer groups.

In summation, the literature establishes that the experience of belonging at work is important—but what is missing is research empirically linking the experience of belonging and performance in the workplace. There is a need for these conversations around belonging; the lack thereof is a problem, not just at a handful of companies or in select industries, but as a widespread issue which we can only hope to eradicate by bringing into the light.

THE SCIENCE OF BELONGING

In 2016, Google's Project Aristotle proved that IQ and resources cannot compensate for an absence of psychological safety. The findings of Project Aristotle are aligned with that which has already been discussed in Chapter 1, that the presence of psychological safety is crucial to belonging. In fact, Google concluded that "psychological safety is the single most important factor contributing to workplace performance."[40]

---

[40] Google, "Guide: Understand Team Effectiveness."

The creation and facilitation of psychological safety is integral to team performance. As we touched on in the section on empathy in Chapter 1, when people feel psychologically safe at work, they can say things like:

- "I don't know."

- "I made a mistake."

- "I disagree."

- "I might be wrong."

- "I am sorry."

- "I have a concern."

- "You are right."

- "I have an idea."

When people don't feel safe, they won't say those things. And if they don't get to say those things, the impact on workplace performance and engagement is clear:

- If you can't share your ideas, that comes at the cost of innovation.

- If you can't say "I don't know," that comes at the cost of expensive errors.

- If you can't say "I might be wrong," that comes at the cost of inviting other people into the conversation.

- If you can't say "I have a concern," that comes at the cost of further wrongdoing that threatens the psychological safety of the team or group.

But, again, when you can say those things, the reverse applies:

- When you can say you have an idea—and that idea is listened to—then you open yourself up to innovation, change, and creativity.

- When you can say "I don't know," you are making yourself available for learning and help.

- When you can say, "I may have made a mistake," you open yourself to fallibility, humanity, and the ability to stop underperforming in the future.

- If you can say, "I disagree," then you open yourself up to the possibility that what you're about to do can be even greater.

Being able to say all of these in one way or another leads to greater cohesion because you're learning from other people. You're communicating your ideas with other people. You are expressing your mistakes and perhaps getting help, again, from other people. You're innovating together. All of this contributes to a sense of connectedness and belonging.

TEAM COHESION

There is an individual's sense of belonging in the workplace, but there is also an individual's sense of belonging within the team they work with. The connectedness we feel with our fellow team members and the psychological safety we feel is also going to support our performance.

The feeling of connectedness, or team cohesion, usually comes about as a result of the team having goal clarity, role clarity, and decision-making clarity—all three of which are inclusionary behaviors.

- Goal clarity helps to establish the why, what, and how of the team: why this team exists, what our measures of success together are, and how we are going to work together in pursuit of those measures of success that will lead back to why we exist as a team. Simon Sinek is a big proponent of starting with why. Then, beyond the why, you clarify what your measures of success are as a team. Finally, you go into your behavioral norms. How are you going to show up as a team?

- After you've established goal clarity, you then establish role clarity: collective awareness to enable responsibility. This is not about job descriptions; role clarity is about understanding the personal attributes each person brings to the team and why they are necessary for the team. It's about understanding how each person will show up in their role and clarity on what each person in that team needs from the others in pursuit of their role.

- Decision-making clarity is about getting clear on what decisions a person can make without collaboration and communication, and what decisions will be made as a team.

When you have team cohesion—everyone feels included, they know their place and everybody else's place, and they accept and can work within that structure—performance has been shown to increase by 50 percent.

Matt Barker, CEO of Planet K2—a group of performance psychologists who work with elite athletes and then translate that work into the world of business, says:

"Connectedness is key to workplace performance. When we are connected, it means that I know who I am, I know who you are, I know how we need to show up together. With connectedness, potential flourishes. When potential flourishes, performance grows." He goes on to explain, "When people belong, they feel at ease. People do their best work when they feel at ease." Additionally, "When people feel like they have a place; when they feel valued for who they are and what they bring—without this, you can never have a high-performance environment."

Barker and his team—which includes Dr. Chris Shambrook, a partner at Planet K2, who has been the psychologist for the British rowing team for many years—understand what it takes to perform in harsh and highly competitive contexts, in conditions which keep changing. The idea of cohesion and connectedness, and therefore belonging, is directly attributable to the performance of athletes and—because the conditions in the world of work are very similar to those of elite athletes—also to workplace performance.

We may not row on the Olympic team or run marathons, but people in the world of work go into the office every day, practice long hours, and attempt to achieve their personal best. We do so in environments that are difficult to perform in, where the contexts are always shifting, and the conditions are always changing. Not only do you have to contend with a client firing you, a global pandemic causing sales to take a nosedive, or a merger or acquisition causing widespread uncertainty—you're also coping with the conditions of your own life. If, when you come to work, you're also experiencing instability in your connectedness and relationships at work, then you have absolutely zero chance of survival.

Connectedness, team cohesion, and belonging are a platform for solid ground in uncertain times. Instead of being blown around by the storm, you become part of the storm—and you harness its power.

SELF-DETERMINATION THEORY

According to Edward Deci and Richard Ryan's work on self-determination theory, people need to feel the following to achieve psychological growth:

- **Autonomy:** People need to feel in control of their own

behaviors and goals. This sense of being able to take direct action that will result in real change plays a major part in helping people feel self-determined.

- **Competence:** People need to gain mastery of tasks and learn different skills. When people feel that they have the skills needed for success, they are more likely to take actions that will help them achieve their goals.

- **Connection or relatedness:** People need to experience a sense of belonging and attachment to other people.[41]

Within self-determination is a seed of self-acceptance. If we can nurture that seed of self-acceptance, that's when we are able to increasingly show up as ourselves. Additionally, if we—as the leaders of companies that individuals work for—are creating places where people can experience autonomy, competence, and connectedness, we are helping those individuals nurture their own self-acceptance and giving everyone a greater chance of belonging.

An individual needs the self-acceptance to be who they are—to bring all of that to the workplace. The workplace needs to foster a place where they can *feel* this sense of belonging.

---

[41] Center for Self-Determination Theory, "The Theory."

A STORY OF
BUILDING CULTURE

JC is a gay, Latino, cisgender male living in the Pacific
Northwest.

BELONGING IN THE WORKPLACE MEANS FEELING SAFE,
respected, and engaged. It means that I don't need to spend
any energy hiding parts of myself and can instead focus on
learning and performing at my peak.

For the first years of my career, in the late eighties and early
nineties, I was closeted because I didn't feel safe coming out
at work. At the time, I was working as the youngest member
of an executive team comprised solely of white men. Though
there were other queer people there, everyone was closeted.
I didn't feel safe. Since I always felt protective of my identity,
I didn't share much of myself there. I felt like a cog in a large
wheel, uninspired to innovate.

The first time that I felt a sense of belonging was working
for MTV Networks in the early nineties, where I was actively
encouraged to be myself. The culture of the organization

was all about bringing out the best of people through openness, creativity, and bringing all voices to the table. The tone
for that culture was set by its leadership, where I also saw
myself reflected as a young, professional, and gay Latino.

I did some of my best work at MTV Networks, and the very
experience of working there is what inspired me to pursue
a career in learning and development and a focus on building culture.

To companies wondering how to build this kind of culture
for themselves, I would say: make sure the benefits you offer
and the policies and procedures you create are designed to
care for the most underrepresented. If you can help those
groups feel a sense of belonging, it's likely others will feel
it too.

As this chapter ends, I would like to offer the following
conclusions:

- **Belonging is important.** Whether viewed through
  the individual, team, or organization lens—or, ideally,

all three—it is impossible to deny the importance of belonging.

- **Belonging is necessary in the workplace.** A sense of belonging contributes to—and is in turn influenced by—a feeling of psychological safety, which allows people to ask for help, admit mistakes, and begin necessary conversations.

- **Belonging is good for workplace performance.** When people experience belonging, they will feel more able to be fully themselves, and they will therefore be freed up to do great work.

Now that we've established the importance of creating a culture of belonging in the workplace, let's take a look at how to create the conditions for that culture to thrive. Chapter 3 shows you how!

CHAPTER 3

CREATING THE CONDITIONS FOR A CULTURE OF BELONGING

*"I personally believe in bringing your
whole self to work and being open and transparent,
even vulnerable. I believe that builds trust, loyalty,
and a sense of belonging and passion."*

—RANA EL KALIOUBY, CEO of Affectiva

> *"It is no longer enough for workplaces to*
> *simply address issues of diversity. We have to go*
> *further so that people from all walks of life not*
> *only see themselves represented at all levels in the*
> *workforce, but they are also having the opportunities*
> *and experiences that lead them to having a seat*
> *at the table where they are influencing the work*
> *being done and the decisions being made."*

—JENNIFER REMLING, author and Global Chief People Officer at WPP

M B is a Filipino, straight, cisgender female in her late thirties who lives and works in Singapore.

I WOULD DEFINE "BELONGING IN THE WORKPLACE" AS fitting into the team and getting a sense that I'm accepted and included in the team's identity. I'm comfortable with the people around me and I can be myself without fear of being judged (well, only to the extent that friends and acquaintances judge each other!).

I have often felt belonging in the places where I've worked, which is why I tend to stay a rather long time in the companies I work with. I worked in Xlibris, later called Author

Solutions, in Cebu, Philippines, and there I felt that I truly belonged within the team. We had close working relationships and great dynamics, which I think led to this positive experience. I wasn't only part of a working team; I eventually felt I was part of a family—one that would look after each other, whether on work-related or personal issues.

When I moved to Essence Singapore, I also felt a strong sense of belonging. Looking around, I saw myself surrounded by like-minded individuals. Relationship-building beyond the work environment also led to people getting to know each other at a personal level and getting to trust that we were more than colleagues but also friends and comrades in arms, so to speak. Getting through some tough times together built camaraderie through adversity. A bond is created when individuals know they can count on someone to understand what they're going through (I guess empathy is the best word here) and also that their team will be there to help them through.

Working for these two companies produced an environment of growth for me. I have benefited from learning from great people and also had the opportunity to impart some of the things I've learned. This creates an atmosphere where there is no need to hoard information and intelligence. Instead, a natural flow of sharing just emanates from people.

We've been able to succeed and do great things, knowing that people have our back. I can say I'm bolder and more adventurous to try things and not afraid to fail knowing that there is a strong team with me. I've also been able to have great relationships even beyond the workplace. Some of the people I've worked with are still close friends.

One of my first jobs, for a real estate company in the Philippines, didn't necessarily make me feel like I belonged. The company was very traditional and protocol-driven, which is not inherently bad, but there was a lot of political play in the office, which led to unnecessary relationship issues and conflict.

Although I worked hard just the same, I often doubted myself. *Was I dressed appropriately? Was I taking the right steps in the process? Was it well documented? Will the boss like it? Will it reflect negatively on other people?* This made the work environment unnecessarily stressful. Although there is often a level of uncertainty at work, this went far beyond what was comfortable, at least for me.

Organizations looking to create the conditions for a culture of belonging should intentionally generate a dynamic environment that allows people to talk to each other and relate at a personal and not just work level. Remember that people aren't just resources; they also have emotional and psychological needs that would benefit the company immensely, if given some attention.

WHAT'S MISSING?

At this point of the book, you now understand the psychological aspects of belonging, and it should be clear that creating a sense of belonging will make your workplace better. In this and the following chapters, we are going to shift gears into examining exactly *how* you can go about creating the conditions for a culture of belonging in your workplace.

But the first question to consider is why this culture *does not already exist* in most companies.

One of the reasons this culture of belonging does not already exist within most companies is due to a lack of empathy and the proclivity to view the world through one's own lens. We all have our own individual experience, and we tend to think that everybody else is having the same experience. However, we all have our own identities and versions of who we are.

In America, we live in an individualistic society—one which places greater emphasis on the individual experience and less on the collective experience—and so we are conditioned into individualism, which can prevent expressions of empathy, curiosity about other people's experiences, and conditions in which *everybody* (not just the person with the most senior job title) can thrive.

Because we also live and work in a capitalistic economy, which drives us to consume, produce, and race and claw our way to the top, our success is measured on how well we do as individuals; it is not measured on how well we do collectively, as a society.

Finally, society is biased toward white, straight, cisgender, able-bodied men. The system is working perfectly because it has been designed to ensure that power stays with those people. Therefore, whenever we try to create the conditions for people who are *not* white, straight, cisgender, able-bodied men to succeed, it rocks the boat—and nobody wants the boat to be rocked when the system is working perfectly.

So why should *you* rock the boat? (Take a look at 2020!) In a capitalistic economy, businesses benefit overall when conditions are created in which *more* people can survive and thrive. And, once again, how do people thrive at work? When they feel a sense of belonging. Thus, we return to what we established in the last chapter: a culture of belonging is good for business.

Bringing it back to this chapter, we are going to look at what you should be measuring to determine whether you have a culture of belonging in your workplace. Then, you will have the opportunity to perform an exercise that can evoke the experience of belonging for you personally. Finally, we will examine the elements necessary to create the conditions for a culture of belonging.

HIGHER SATISFACTION, LOWER ATTRITION

I worked at an ad agency called Essence, where I was the chief learning and culture officer for eight years and then the chief advisor to the CEO for a year. In that role, I worked with the chief talent officer and the CEO on our diversity, inclusion, and belonging plan. It lowered attrition amongst our underrepresented and historically disempowered communities and increased morale and satisfaction.

Two of the most important people metrics, aside from individual performance, are your rates of attrition and satisfaction. And there is a correlation between the two: the higher the satisfaction, the lower the attrition.

In general, organizations operating from an individualistic, capitalist (and often patriarchal) perspective tend to measure —perhaps unsurprisingly—key performance indicators (KPIs) around individual performance or profit. While those remain important indicators of a company's performance, it is also necessary to measure attrition and satisfaction. People are leaving for a reason—and, on the flip side—people are *staying* for a reason, too. When you shift from focusing solely on performance and therefore profitability, revenue, and market share, you can discover the reason people may want to leave —and implement the changes that help people feel comfortable staying.

Attrition is fairly straightforward to measure, and there are many solutions around measuring employee satisfaction and engagement.

Although it is inherently flawed and challenging to measure revenue and profits in relation to diversity, inclusion, and belonging, there is tons of research that talks about the correlation between attrition and satisfaction and how high levels of employee satisfaction drive KPIs like productivity, profitability, and client happiness.

THE EXPERIENCE OF BELONGING

From what I can tell from my own experience and from listening to the experiences of my coaching clients, clinical patients, and colleagues over the years, belonging is not just an emotional event; it is a cognitive, somatic, and sometimes spiritual experience.

To understand this a little more, I want to ask you to try out a little experiment with me. It goes like this:

- Think of a one-time event in your past in which you knew you belonged. It could be in a workplace, within your family of origin, perhaps within your chosen family. Maybe it was at school. It could even be a sublime moment of alone time while sitting on the couch watching Netflix with a bowl of Doritos,[42] binge-watching your favorite show (a.k.a. self-care).

---

[42] Other snacks are available.

- Make sure it is a one-time event. And make sure that you think of an event in which you knew you *absolutely* belonged.

- In your mind's eye, make a picture of this event. See yourself in this picture, belonging.

- Now, I want you to float yourself into your body in the picture so that you are looking through your own eyes. You should now be in your own body in the picture, experiencing yourself belonging in this one-time event.

  - Notice what you see.

  - Notice what you hear.

  - Notice your feelings or emotions.

  - Notice what's happening in your body. Notice any sensations, vibrations, or warmth. Notice what's happening in terms of movement and gestures. Notice any tastes. And I would like you to pay particular attention to any smells you notice.

  - Now, notice your thoughts or internal dialogue.

- When you are done noticing, float out of the picture and bring yourself back to the here and now.

How was that? Were you able to notice how belonging is so much more than a feeling? It involves all the senses, which is why I refer to belonging as an *experience*.

BELONGING DOESN'T EXIST WITHOUT DIVERSITY PLUS INCLUSION

It's important when thinking about facilitating belonging in the workplace to remember that while inclusivity is a prerequisite for belonging and diversity is a prerequisite for inclusivity, a diverse workforce won't always lead to inclusive behaviors and inclusive behaviors won't always lead to the experience of belonging.

A company can take action to recruit a diverse workforce—yet if the systems, policies, procedures, and behaviors of the workforce are not inclusive, then the so-called diverse hires[43] that the company has made will soon tire of not feeling included—and they will likely leave, which ultimately negates the efforts made in increasing diversity and representation. If a company wants to cultivate an environment in which people feel like

---

[43] Diverse hires: The practice or policy of recruiting individuals belonging to groups known to have been discriminated against previously.

they belong,[44] leaders must first address issues of diversity and then they must put in place policies, processes, and practices that encourage inclusive behaviors.

The following table presents a range of methods in which a company can tackle issues of diversity and inclusion and, in doing so, pave the way for the experience of belonging.[45]

ADDRESSING DIVERSITY	FACILITATING INCLUSION
Targets and transparent reporting	Cultural fabric
Hiring manager education	Policy and procedure
Diverse talent pipelining	Premises and built environment
Diverse slate recruitment	Employee resource groups
Equal access screening	Education and training
Culture add versus culture fit interviews	Safe rooms and brave spaces

---

[44] I think, by now, we have established a case for belonging. But just in case we need to review: a workplace in which people experience belonging is better than a workplace in which people feel like they do not belong.

[45] This table has been developed through my own experience as an HR professional, clinician, and coach, along with research and interviews with industry specialists including Amanda Schmidt, a chief people officer at Dept Agency; Dan Sullivan, a global leader in architecture and the built environment; Dawn Barker, a chief HR officer from the UK; Jennifer Remling, author of *Care Your Own Road* and a chief people officer at WPP; Katie Farber, a global leader in talent acquisition; and Lindsey Wells, a diversity and inclusion recruitment director from New York City.

Each of these methods will represent a section of the upcoming Chapters 4 and 5, about addressing diversity and facilitating inclusion, respectively.

A STORY OF COMPANY CULTURE

SC is a white, straight, cisgender female in her early forties who lives and works in Montreal, Quebec.

IN THE EARLY 2000S, I WORKED FOR A TOP ADVERTISING agency in London. Everybody else came from Oxbridge and joined via the graduate scheme, whereas I joined as a PA and worked my way up—a fact that was never forgotten and, I felt, always held against me. The staff were incredibly un-diverse: very few women in senior positions, and when the recession came, senior women with children lost their jobs first. I couldn't see myself having any future there. My direct manager was snide at first, and looking back, I believe her behavior would be classified as workplace bullying. Senior management promoted a culture of drinking, drugs, and endless work. I remember watching one senior female manager leaving to attend her daughter's carol concert and making a point of the fact that she would leave it if she was needed, that her phone would be on all the time. There was no sense of work–life balance, and it was dog-eat-dog.

Every day when I went into work, I felt physically ill. I lost confidence, stopped standing up for myself, and didn't dispute when my manager put me on probation. I didn't care—I was working twelve- to sixteen-hour days regularly and getting sick all the time because I was so tired and unhappy.

The turning point for me was when I realized that the issue was my manager and her attitude, not me. I worked the probation, was recognized for doing a good job by the rest of the team, and resigned on my terms.

Although my experiences since have been positive, I still to this day feel sick when I think of my old manager. It was clear to the other employees what she was doing—and indeed, one of them subsequently apologized to me for not having stood up for me—but nobody would have dreamt of doing anything because in that environment, you were either with them, or against them. There was no room for diversity of opinion.

After that, I went to work for a travel/transport company, where I felt a sense of alignment with the overall mission. That sense of belonging became even stronger over time as my personal life came to reflect the cross-cultural mission of the company. When there was disagreement, it was almost always with a view to achieving something better, rather than territorial.

I was coming out of a very negative stage in my life and career, and having a supportive and inspiring boss and colleagues who were similar in age and life-stage to me felt like coming home. I felt empowered to try new things, to get it wrong from time to time, and my increased personal confidence spilled over into all areas of my life. However, that also made it very hard for me to move on from the company, to the extent that I stayed beyond the point I probably should have. I also recognize now, after talking to ex-colleagues there of different ethnic backgrounds, that my experience of belonging and identifying was probably also rooted in aspects that made their sense of belonging more challenging.

To me, a culture of belonging in the workplace is created when you feel that your values and those of the company are aligned in some way, that what they want to achieve for their business is something that you can contribute toward and be proud of. Lately, I would also add: doing business in an ethical manner that feels consistent with my values. I think there's also an aspect related to progression: if you feel that you can't progress in an organization, then inherently you see it as a short-term stay, rather than somewhere that invests in you and where you are similarly invested in the future of the company.

My advice is to be clear on your expectations. Don't expect everybody to perform in the same way, because everybody will bring something different to the table; and reward good management—this is really the unsung skill in most companies.

As this chapter ends, I would like to offer the following conclusions:

- **There are KPIs you can measure to gain a sense of your company's culture of belonging.** It is important to measure both attrition and satisfaction, because the higher the satisfaction, the lower your attrition rates will be.

- **Belonging is an experience.** When you experience (or reflect on) belonging personally, it becomes easier to see the path to creating that experience for others.

- **Belonging is only possible when you first have diversity and inclusion.** Without diversity, inclusion is impossible—and without inclusion, the experience of belonging cannot be achieved.

You've had a preview of the conditions that will allow a culture of belonging to flourish in your workplace. The first factor is to address diversity, which is the topic of Chapter 4.

ADDRESSING
DIVERSITY

"Until you make the unconscious conscious,
it will direct your life and you
will call it fate."

—CARL JUNG

E H is a white, queer, cis woman in her late twenties who lives and works in Portland, Oregon.

I THINK OF BELONGING IN TWO WAYS. FIRST, THAT YOU feel a sense of individual attunement, safety, and resonance enough to share ideas and passions as well as concerns and troubles. Second, I think of a sort of web or interdependence—that there is a sense that you are part of the group in such a way that you are both relied on and can rely on others for support. Contrary to the pressure to produce in American work culture, I only feel belonging when it feels like there is space for me to not always be working, producing, and creating. Finally, I think it is very hard to really feel belonging when there is a very apparent power structure and hierarchy.

My current internship is one of the few places I've truly felt belonging. I am a counseling intern at META Counseling Clinic, which is part of a Hakomi training center. I feel able to be fully myself in my growth process, even if it is not always "productive." Growth and learning is the point; support is the means. There is always space and invitation to ask if help is needed. There is a culture of showing up just as you are, and of receiving others just as they are. There is an openness for the trainees to be creating the work culture and changing the systems of the clinic, though there is a base structure and environment to guide us. There is spaciousness. I also want to name that META is a primarily white space, with mainly AFAB[46] and queer folx,[47] and I know this contributes to my sense of belonging. Additionally, I think the fact that the experience does not push outcomes, but instead more our growth as therapists, is key.

In contrast, I worked for two small, women-owned floral companies where I felt less like a person to be invested in and more like a tool in the movement of the company. Though there was kindness, and sometimes even friendship, I primarily felt like a workhorse. It seemed that responsibilities were either withheld because of the owner's desire to control, or I was given too many responsibilities with not enough training or support so the owner could step back. Both jobs ended in ways where I felt like I had put my time, body, emotions, and hopes into someone else's project and

---

[46] AFAB: Assigned female at birth. When people are born, they are assigned a gender based on their sex genitalia. If you have a penis, you are assigned by the doctors as being male and you are from there on known as a "boy" and are assumed to be, do, and have all the characteristics of boys. If you are born with a vulva, you are assigned female, called a "girl" and in the same way as little boys, a range of assumptions about you tend to get made. If you are born with ambiguous genitalia (about 1.7 percent of the population is born as what is medically known as "intersex"), the doctors are required to assign you a sex and from there on that little person, just like other little people, experiences the same social pressure to conform, act, and show up in the world with the characteristics of the gender they were assigned at birth.

[47] Folx: An alternative spelling to the word "folks." The spelling has been adopted by some communities because it can be used to indicate inclusion of marginalized groups.

had not much to show for it at the end. I worked very hard at these jobs, but never was able to feel good about what I had accomplished.

I think so much of work culture is inherently dehumanizing. We are so outcome- and production-oriented that our humanity goes out the window—fast.

Some ideas that come to mind for building a culture of belonging are, first, frankly, decentering whiteness, cis-male-ness, and other privilege-holding normative identities. Our system of hiring diversity coordinators does not work because there is no way of bringing in diversity from a center of whiteness etc. without marginalizing within the company/organization.

I also think that workplaces are often either struggling to survive or are so growth- and profit-oriented that they forget or don't see that investing in your employees benefits the company. It is the job of the people on top to normalize not working crazy hours and taking care of yourself, your family, and your community. Workplaces need to be invested in their employees, even beyond their work together.

BUT FIRST . . . WHY?

Before exploring the ways in which companies can address diversity and rebalancing representation in their workforces, I want to spend a moment discussing *why* companies should address the issue. John Biewen in the *Scene on Radio* podcast series *MEN* and *Seeing White* tells the story of the origins of American and British societies favoring certain characteristics and phenotypes[48] and dividing these characteristics and phenotypes into "good," "better," "bad," and "lesser," and then building systems of power in favor of those who made it into the categories of "good" and "better."

Even though science has shown us that there is no biological basis for these categorizations to exist, through the ongoing social conditioning of humans during our development, these categories have prevailed and the biases toward these groups have deepened and taken hold generationally. These biases continue to play out and exert an influence—overtly and covertly—in every aspect of our society and our decision-making.

---

[48] Phenotype: The set of observable characteristics (such as skin color) of an individual resulting from the interaction of their genotype with the environment.

It is not within the scope of this book to fully unpack the whys and wherefores that have led to us establishing what I have referred as the "dominant group" and the "subordinate group." Needless to say, it takes deliberate, willful, conscious action to mitigate the biases that exist as a result of centuries of social conditioning that has shown favor to the dominant group.

Diversity in the workplace is a fact. It is a function of representation in that it occurs when people from different walks of life are present in a group or team. For example, when a Black, working class, transgender, millennial, overweight woman looks up, down, or to the side of themself in their workplace, do they see any of their identities reflected back at them or do they see people who are mostly white, cisgender, able-bodied, generation X, middle-class, thin, or males? They either do or they do not. There either is diversity or there is not.

The only way, without exception, to establish diversity in the workplace is to increase the number of people who have identities that are different to the identities held by the dominant group. Many organizations refer to this as "affirmative action"[49] and the people recruited as "diverse hires."

---

[49] Affirmative action: Based on merit with special care taken to ensure procedures are free from biases related to a candidate's age, race, gender, religion, sexual orientation, and other personal characteristics that are unrelated to their job performance.

What follows are some thoughts and ideas as to how establish diversity in your organization. As you will see, each section reflects on an item in the first column of the table of creating a culture of belonging in the workplace:

ADDRESSING DIVERSITY	FACILITATING INCLUSION
Targets and transparent reporting	Cultural fabric
Hiring manager education	Policy and procedure
Diverse talent pipelining	Premises and built environment
Diverse slate recruitment	Employee resource groups
Equal access screening	Education and training
Culture add versus culture fit interviews	Safe rooms and brave spaces

TARGETS AND TRANSPARENT REPORTING

The old adage "what gets measured gets managed" is truly applicable in the space of addressing diversity. I personally believe that a workforce should be representative of the communities in which a company trades and/or the customer base they target or serve. National and regional sex, race, ethnicity, and disability population figures are provided by government and local councils in most countries and regions, so it should be straightforward enough for a company to hold itself accountable for establishing a workforce that mirrors this data. It is less straightforward to set targets around LGBTQIA2+ and gender identity representation because of the challenges associated with collecting the data in the first place, but this can be addressed through talent pipelining approaches, which will be discussed in a later section.

I also believe that it is important for a company to publish its targets internally and externally as a way of keeping itself accountable. Publishing targets internally demonstrates to employees that diversity and inclusion are a priority and at the same time articulates expectation to its leaders. Publishing externally helps prospective employees make conscious choices about companies where they do, or do not, wish to work.

Of course, publishing the targets is just a first step. Without transparently communicating about the progress (or lack thereof) toward the targets,[50] employees may well start to believe that diversity and inclusion initiatives have been a flash-in-the-pan or flavor-of-the-month.

---

[50] I cannot emphasize enough the impact of honesty and transparency when it comes to communicating lack of progress. People from nondominant groups tend to be adept at seeing through any "smoke and mirrors" (i.e., the obscuring or embellishing of the truth of a situation with misleading or irrelevant information) due to a lifetime of oppression and marginalization.

HIRING MANAGER
EDUCATION

A number of tweets, blogs, and articles have emerged this year to shine a light on job postings that require unrealistic levels of experience. It would seem that everyone is looking for a purple unicorn[51] and in doing so are chasing away some of the best candidates.

Katie Farber, a global leader in talent acquisition, told me that she encourages her hiring managers to think about transferable skills and adjacent (rather than same-industry) experience when seeking new members to join their team. Farber also told me that she thinks it is the responsibility for the talent acquisition community to mitigate the inevitable impact of hiring managers' unconscious biases and said, "We have to lean in and help shine a light on biases and unrealistic requirements when we see them," arguing for recruiters to play a proactive role in educating and partnering with their hiring managers from a diversity perspective.

---

[51] "Purple unicorn" is a term used to describe a candidate profile that possesses skills and experiences that are believed to be so rare, they are almost mythical.

DIVERSE
TALENT PIPELINING

As humans, we inherently have biases that operate at an unconscious level. There are four major classifications of unconscious bias:

- **Affinity bias:** The tendency of people to connect with others who share similar interests, experiences, and backgrounds.

- **Confirmation bias:** The inclination to draw conclusions about a situation or person based on your own personal beliefs or prejudices.

- **Attribution bias:** A phenomenon whereby you judge a person's behavior based on previous experiences you've had with them.

- **Conformity bias:** The tendency of people to act in similar ways to the people around them, regardless of their own personal beliefs; this is another term for peer pressure.

If you are a recruiter or hiring manager, these biases are at play in the recruitment process. They just are, as a fact; you're never going to escape that. I'll use myself as an example: I am a queer, nonbinary, white, male-bodied person. If I am not aware of the biases I have around that identity, then guess what? I'm going to go out and recruit people who look more like me—without doing so intentionally—because my biases influence my perception of who fits the bill and who does not.

The only way to address your unconscious biases is to do the work of understanding what those biases are, so that you can be aware of that influence when you're making decisions.

From there, you can move toward making sure that more people can see the jobs you have available—giving you the opportunity for a more diverse hiring pool, rather than the same old, same old.

"You cannot hire diverse talent if diverse talent [isn't] applying for jobs. We have to take opportunities to the communities that wouldn't normally see the opportunities." So says Lindsey Wells, a diversity recruitment director, highlighting the need for filling the sourcing pipeline with people from diverse backgrounds. To achieve this, Wells advocates for two things:

1. Collaborating with external organizations/taskforces (for example, Out in Tech, She Runs It, MAIP, and the Thurgood Marshall Foundation), as well as sourcing from specific community groups on LinkedIn.

2. Truth and authenticity, noting that while some recruiters might not want to say to candidates, "We want to hire you not only because you are great but also because of your identity," Wells' experience tells her that this level of truth tends to be well-received and is an important ingredient to candidates feeling safe[r] in coming to an interview.

Wells also shared with me an email template that she has been using in her outreach work:

Hello,

I hope you're staying well during these unusual times.

My name is Lindsey and I've been in my role for over two years recruiting diverse talent across all levels at <insert organization name>. Like so many places, we are working on increasing our Black and Brown representation[52] across all levels of our business.

---

[52] Wells tailors this depending on the community she is reaching out to.

We are hiring for a <insert job title> to work on our <insert team name> and looking at your skills and experience, I think you might be a great fit. If you're open and willing to talk, let me know your availability.

This practice of diverse talent pipelining (and the next section, "Blank Slate Recruitment") is designed to counteract the impact of unconscious biases by taking job opportunities to the communities that wouldn't normally be made aware of them, in ways they may not typically see them. If you only run an ad on LinkedIn, what about the people who aren't on LinkedIn? How are you going to reach professional people who don't want to go on social media at all?

This requires first recognizing your own unconscious biases when you are interviewing and making the selection. But it also requires recognizing that you have traditionally taken job opportunities to a specific community or communities and, therefore, your talent pool is homogenous.

DIVERSE SLATE RECRUITMENT

In a previous section, I talked about the importance of building teams and companies that reflect the diversity of the communities in which they do business and the customer bases that they serve. Both Farber and Wells agree, and in their work, they have committed to delivering to hiring managers what they call a "Diverse Slate." This means that at least 50 percent of the longlist of candidates they present to hiring managers consists of people from the nondominant group.

Once you have people applying for jobs who are from historically disempowered or marginalized communities—in other words, diverse hires, people who look different from the rest of your workforce—then you have to go through another level of mitigation against unconscious biases.

I worked with a group of people at an advertising agency who said they had declined somebody for a job because the applicant *wore a suit* to the interview and they couldn't see themselves wanting to have a drink with that applicant in the bar after work.

What that group of people was essentially saying was, "That prospective hire probably won't fit in." But the idea that "they won't fit in" is exactly the problem! Blank slate recruitment and diverse talent pipelining (and, again, the next section on equal access screening) are designed to counteract that exact sentiment.

EQUAL ACCESS SCREENING

Iris Bohnet, Director of the Women and Public Policy Program at the Harvard Kennedy School and author of *What Works: Gender Equality by Design* says, "The fact is a Latisha or a Jamal do not get the same number of callbacks as an Emily or a Greg," and that "going blind" on demo- and bio-graphic data (such as names, gender, addresses, and colleges attended) during the interview process can help to remove prejudice and ensure that more diverse candidates make it from the longlist to the shortlist after resume review.[53]

Soll, Milkman, and Payne agree and refer to this process as a way to "outsmart your own biases" and avoid what they call "System 1 thinking," which drives automatic judgments stemming from associations stored in memory (i.e., biases) rather than logically working through the information that's available.[54]

---

[53] Knight, "7 Practical Ways to Reduce Bias in Your Hiring Process: Start by Reworking Your Job Descriptions."

[54] Soll, Milkman, and Payne, "Outsmart Your Own Biases: How to Broaden Your Thinking and Make Better Decisions."

CULTURE ADD VERSUS CULTURE FIT INTERVIEWING

In the early 2000s and 2010s, there was a big wave of assuming that "as long as recruits will succeed in our culture, we can train them on the skills and knowledge." But this mindset further exacerbates the homogenous workforce. When you go for culture fit, you're going to bring in more people who are not going to challenge the status quo, ask difficult questions, or think differently about the same topics all business face; you get a herd mentality. It tells people to prioritize fitting in over bringing their authentic selves to the workplace. (Lest you think I'm exaggerating, these messages are out there: companies advertising their culture on their career pages and showing pictures of happy employees are demonstrating the type of people they want. Many companies will even have a culture-fit interview as part of their interview selection process.)

On this topic, Farber speaks of the need for companies to move from "culture fit" to "culture add" interviews, saying that the culture fit selection process encourages the growth of homogenous teams and plays into biases by finding "people like us."

Focusing on culture *add*, on the other hand, encourages hiring managers to ask potential employees, "What are you going to bring that we don't currently have? How do you see yourself innovating or creating change here? What would you change about this industry?" You're asking them to bring their natural talents and skills to bear for the good and growth of the company; you're not asking them to show up and be just like everyone else.

One way Farber approaches this is by involving members of employee resource groups in the interviewing team so that there is someone outside of the hiring team involved in the recruitment process. She asserts that it remains crucial that candidates align with, and can uphold, a company's cultural fabric. At the same time, she encourages the hiring team to ask themselves questions such as, "What does this person bring that is new, unique, and that nobody else has?" or (while recognizing that there is no such thing as a purple unicorn) "Can this person be successful in this role if we provide them with the right support and training?"

Steve Jobs once said, "It doesn't make sense to hire smart people and tell them what to do." My counterpoint to that would be: **it doesn't make sense to hire brilliant people and tell them how to *be*.** It makes more sense to hire brilliant people and create an environment that allows them to fully unleash their creativity for the good of the business.

A STORY OF DIVERSITY

AV is an Indian, straight, cisgender male in his early thirties who lives and works in New Delhi.

AN ORGANIZATION MAY HAVE A DIVERSE REPRESENTA-tion but may still not be inclusive. And if they are not inclusive, the feeling of "belonging" may still be missing amongst employees. To me, the feeling of belonging comes when employees can bring their own authentic selves to the workplace, aren't judged for the background they come from (education, previous experience, contractor or permanent status, etc.), and feel valued and that their opinions matter.

I felt this sense of belonging during one of my stints at my previous company, posted at Chennai, India. Even though I was a North Indian working in South India (where the culture differs in terms of food, habits, language, and even behavior), I was never made to feel like an outsider. I never had to worry whether I would be misunderstood by my colleagues, and I was always asked for my opinion on important decisions. My manager took efforts to ensure

I felt at home in the new city, trusted me with bigger responsibilities, rewarded me with challenging work, helped me grow in my career, and made me a better people manager.

All this made me feel like I did not want to let my manager and the entire team down. I was proud of my work, and I tried instilling that feeling in all my team members. I was given the highest rating for all the years I spent there, received a couple of promotions, and had the opportunity to work abroad at the company's global headquarters. I felt very confident about everything I was doing and it reflected in my conversations with the colleagues across locations.

Ironically, I felt the loss of my sense of belonging at the same company when I moved into a new role I hadn't done before. I would like to say that, being new to the role, I for sure didn't have a complete grasp over things I was expected to do. And as much as I was told by my manager that she believed in me, it was not reflected in the actions she—or the rest of the team—took. I was occasionally subjected to snide remarks and compared with junior colleagues. I wasn't in the top ratings anymore, which I took as a learning experience for myself, but I didn't feel happy or valued at work.

To build diversity and belonging, I would say that if you've chosen an employee, back them up and trust them, irrespective of the work background they come with. Make them feel that they can voice their opinion, even if wrong, and correct them when needed. Instill confidence in them, give them room to run, and help them learn the ropes. Give constructive feedback but ensure the day-to-day actions don't unintentionally hinder their confidence and morale.

As this chapter ends, I would like to offer the following conclusions:

- **Diversity is important.** Without a diverse workplace— which requires diverse job candidates—inclusion and belonging cannot exist.

- **We all have unconscious biases.** Our biases lead us to surround ourselves with people who are similar to us; it is only by acknowledging these biases that we can work to overcome them.

- **Fitting in is not as important as being yourself.**
  A company that emphasizes fitting in is going to
  have a less diverse workforce than one that focuses
  on what individual hires can bring by being their
  authentic selves.

Katie Farber once said that "a lot of this should not be considered frosting on the cake. It *is* the cake."

Since we've talked about the cake, let's now talk about the frosting: inclusion.

CHAPTER 5

FACILITATING INCLUSION

"When everyone is included,
everyone wins."

—JESSE JACKSON

J H is an Asian-American, straight, cisgender man in his late thirties who lives and works in Minneapolis, Minnesota.

TO ME, BELONGING IS A FEELING OF BEING ACTIVELY heard and supported, with equal visibility into the conditions of the workplace.

When I first joined my current company in June of 2016, it was still a digital-only media agency that was part of a collective group of agencies designed to service our client in Minneapolis, with a larger team located in New York. Even though we were a satellite presence at the time, I could really feel the spirit of the company; its passion for smart, rigorous thinking and candid communication from all levels of leadership came through.

It was refreshing to have leaders within an organization who could speak candidly but intelligently about the company. They were able to contextualize news about or around the company to help me understand the big picture and how it may or may not impact my immediate role. That combination really helped me keep a well-balanced perspective overall and motivated me to execute well and continue to learn.

However, after some organizational changes took place in 2018, I haven't felt like I belonged any longer. The biggest factor was the absorption of external team members into the company. These individuals, including those in leadership positions, were part of a team that focused on nondigital media investment. The side effects of this became a reprioritization of how we serviced our client, specifically a perceived shift from the digital expertise that our company had been known for to more of a traditional media focus due to the size of investment.

As a digital expert, while my immediate role hasn't changed, the significance of my role has been reduced. In addition, resulting leadership changes have created the following experiences for me:

1. Being pigeon-holed as a digital expert and not being recognized for my broad spectrum of media knowledge.

2. Information sharing became limited to prioritize certain individuals rather than candidly communicating to the broader team in equity. For example, criteria for upward movement on my immediate position is not public knowledge and kept to certain individuals.

3. Since 2018, my efforts to define my next role have been stifled, with no perceivable support from leadership while clear paths have been created for other members on the team.

My baseline performance is always there—meeting my core responsibilities and making the most out of what's in front of me. However, a lot of projects that I had taken on, in addition to my core remit that I thought would help pave the way to my next role, have not come to fruition. I still take those on, but seeing the developments around me and lack thereof, for me, has made it difficult.

INCLUSION GIVES A GREATER CHANCE FOR BELONGING

If our formula says that diversity plus inclusion can equal belonging, we are now at the second stage: inclusion. Again, where diversity is a fact, inclusion is the set of behaviors that can be instilled, which will give your organization the greatest chance of leading to belonging.

I again want to emphasize that you must have diversity to have inclusion, and you must have inclusion to have belonging. You can do everything we laid out in Chapter 4, but if you skip this chapter, you will not have inclusion—and thus, you *certainly* are guaranteed not to have belonging.

It is also important to note that diversity doesn't always lead to belonging. Similarly, inclusion doesn't always lead to belonging—but with the topics in this chapter, you have a greater chance of facilitating inclusive behaviors that can create the experience of belonging within your organization.

The sections in this chapter are reflected in the right-hand column of the table for creating a culture of belonging in the workplace:

ADDRESSING DIVERSITY	FACILITATING INCLUSION
Targets and transparent reporting	Cultural fabric
Hiring manager education	Policy and procedure
Diverse talent pipelining	Premises and built environment
Diverse slate recruitment	Employee resource groups
Equal access screening	Education and training
Culture add versus culture fit interviews	Safe rooms and brave spaces

CULTURAL FABRIC

As described in Chapter 2, "cultural fabric" is the collective noun I use to describe the wiring that powers a stated and intended organizational culture.

Your company's cultural fabric is the map that drives and creates the explicit culture and also helps to shape the implicit climate. Culture describes the way you want your organization to behave, and the climate is the way in which employees experience how the company really is.

The cultural fabric starts to provide a foundation from which we can articulate the experience we want people to have of working in the company—which, by the way, may or may not end up being the experience they *actually* have. But it at least sets out a clear intention for the employee experience, and from that, you then get to design people policies, practices, processes, and interventions that bring that people philosophy (and experiences) to life.

If inclusion is not embedded into that cultural fabric, then chances are, it's not going to be consciously thought about when it comes to the process of designing the people experience. If, however, inclusion is a conscious part of your culture in the process of designing the people experience, then there exists a far greater chance of belonging being an experience that people have.

INCLUSIVE EMPLOYMENT POLICIES AND PROCEDURES

A company's employment policies dictate, to a significant extent, how inclusive a workplace will be for employees.[55]

This is not meant to be an exhaustive list, but here are some topics that a company can consider to make their employment practices more inclusive:

- **Flexible working practices,** which enable people with families or employees who are taking care of dependents to work while fulfilling their duties at home.

- It is important to eliminate heteronormativity from **parental leave policies** by ensuring they do not delineate on the basis of sex or gender nor use the

---

[55] Best practice information on inclusive employment practices are available online at https://www.shrm.org/, https://www.cipd.co.uk/, https://www.stonewall.org.uk/, and https://www.hrc.org/.

words "mother" or "father." It is preferable instead to use "parent" or "primary caregiver."

- **Pronouns and preferred name.** On the surface, this might seem like an education issue rather than a matter of policy. With that said, oftentimes a company's email address policy will be based on an employee's legal name and legal gender-assigned-at-birth.[56] Without a policy on the use of pronouns and preferred names, companies may fail to recognize an individual's gender identity, which can constitute a violation of harassment and discrimination laws in some countries and territories. Even in geographies where there is no law supporting this topic, companies would be advised to adopt an inclusive approach on this incredibly personal topic.

- Establish a **transgender policy** which supports trans individuals in their social and medical transition at work. According to the Transgender Law Center, at a minimum, this policy should lay out guidelines that cover the right to privacy, handling of official records,

---

[56] An employee's online profile is inextricably linked to their company email address, which in turn has a significant impact on their professional personas and identity. Ensuring an employee can be emailed at their chosen name is a crucial part of being an inclusive employer.

healthcare, and benefits, how to approach sex-segregated job duties, support during transition and through gender confirmation surgery (if the individual elects to have surgery), restroom and locker room accessibility, dress codes, and the process of recourse if transgender individuals experience harassment or discrimination at work.

PREMISES AND BUILT ENVIRONMENT

Features of inclusive work environments range from physical aspects to less-permanent attributes. For example:

- The provision of all-gender bathrooms.[57]

- Ramps and aisle spaces wide enough for wheelchair users.

- Ensuring menstrual products are available in all bathrooms so that trans and nonbinary people have access to them.

---

[57] I purposefully use the phrase "all-gender" to represent the spectrum of gender identities that exist.

- Signage in font sizes and colors that support those who have challenges with their visual senses.

- Use of different technologies to support those who are deaf or hard of hearing.

- In Dan Sullivan's words, the importance of driving equity for neurodiverse people in the workplace by "recognizing how certain patterns can be especially distracting for these folks, or how wayfinding needs to be addressed for them, or how we can help facilitate or ease task-switching for these types of brains through what we introduce in the workplace."

In 2008, the UK's Commission for Architecture for the Built Environment Design Council published a paper that opened with the words,

The quality of buildings and spaces has a strong influence on the quality of people's lives. Decisions about the design, planning, and management of places can enhance or restrict a sense of belonging. They can increase or reduce feelings of security, stretch or limit boundaries, promote or reduce mobility, and improve or damage health. They can remove real and imagined barriers between communities and foster understanding and generosity of spirit.[58]

EMPLOYEE RESOURCE GROUPS (ERGS)

Employee resource groups, or ERGs, are typically organized around a shared identity, such as race, gender, sexual orientation, age, or mental health and serve as a haven of belonging, offering a space for underrepresented employees[59] to find community and experience a reprieve from the daily micro-aggressions they've likely endured at work. ERGs can provide much-needed education and awareness-raising to the broader organization.

According to a 2014 survey conducted by Software Advice, 70 percent of US respondents who were eighteen to twenty-four years old and 52 percent of respondents between twenty-five and thirty-four reported they would be more likely to apply for a role at a company that had ERGs. Additionally, 50 percent

---

[58] Commission for Architecture and the Built Environment, *Inclusion by Design: Equality, Diversity and the Built Environment.*

[59] Anyone else curious as to why we don't see the word "overrepresented" used in relation to the dominant group?

of survey respondents stated they would remain at a company because it had an ERG.[60]

A word of warning though: in my personal experience, it is not enough for a company to simply give permission to its underrepresented groups to start an ERG. The most successful ERGs—the ones that drive greatest community, facilitate broad company-wide education about the underrepresented, and provide safe havens for minority people—have a budget, executive support, and participation from employees who do not share identities with the ERG community (a.k.a. active participation of allies).

Rebekah Bastian, a contributor for *Forbes* who writes about culture, equity, and belonging in the workplace, agrees and says that "while some ERGs may start as grassroots efforts, those that have the support of company leadership can be more impactful for employees. Formal support can result in permanent ERG program budgets to spend on programming for their members, support for employees to use work hours on group activities, and open communication channels for them to influence business decisions."[61]

---

[60] Kruse, "Are You Engaged at Work? The Importance of Friendship and Employee Resource Groups."

[61] Bastian, "How to Foster Workplace Belonging Through Successful Employee Resource Groups."

EDUCATION AND TRAINING

When I was interviewing her, Lindsey Wells said to me, "Managers can really affect your career path and how you show up for others at work," and in doing so echoed the words of Marcus Buckingham and Curt Coffman who, in their 1999 book, *First, Break All the Rules,*[62] famously concluded that "people don't leave bad companies; they leave bad managers." This serves to emphasize how important it is that companies educate their managers in how to lead their teams in an inclusive manner.

One important area of inclusivity education and training is in learning how to move from being a bystander to an up-stander, from an ally to an accomplice.

A bystander is a well-intended onlooker who hears or witnesses microaggressions but doesn't do anything about it. They don't join in, but they also don't challenge it. They are an uninvolved witness who doesn't do anything. An up-stander, on the other

---

[62] *First, Break All the Rules* has been named one of the twenty-five most influential business books of all time. The book is a result of observations based on 80,000 interviews with managers as conducted by the Gallup Organization across twenty-five years. The core of the matter lies in how these managers have debunked old myths about management and how they created new truths on obtaining and keeping talented people in their organization.

hand, calls people out on their microaggressions. For example, a white person would call out another white person on their racial microaggressions, and a straight person would call out another straight person on their heterosexist microaggressions. An up-stander uses their unearned identity privilege when they hear or witness microaggressions happening.

There is a similar difference between being an ally and being an accomplice. An ally is a person from a nonmarginalized group who uses their privilege to advocate for those who have historically disempowered identity markers. So, whereas an up-stander is someone who intervenes when they see or hear a microaggression happening, an ally actively works at decentering themselves and centering other people in the conversation. A straight ally, for example, would invite a queer person into the place where the decisions are being made, where they would otherwise not be welcomed.

An accomplice is even a step on from that, a person from a nonmarginalized group who uses their unearned privilege to dismantle the structures and systems that oppress the individuals or groups. In an individualistic capitalist society where the system is working perfectly (as we explored in Chapter 3), an accomplice would be a person who works at dismantling those structures that distribute power solely to white, straight, cis-het men.

At a minimum, inclusive practices should involve training in understanding and exploring unconscious bias, but I think we need to go much further than this. I'm advocating for companies to invite their employees (not just leaders) into learning spaces that facilitate dialogue and education about the experience of minority and oppressed communities inside and outside of the workplace.[63]

SAFE ROOMS AND INTENTIONALLY BRAVE SPACES

In an earlier chapter, I discussed the conundrum we face when we—particularly people from the dominant group—name spaces as being safe for people to show up and participate. Instead, I encourage companies to consider the creation of either "safe rooms" or "intentionally brave spaces," in which the delicate (and oftentimes messy) conversations that are necessary for processing complex trauma and the harm inflicted by systemic oppression and day-to-day microaggressions can take place.

---

[63] I facilitate a training that managers, leaders, and employees can take to learn more about the differences between bystanders, up-standers, allies, and accomplices, and how to use this information to further develop inclusivity in the workplace. More about that in the Conclusion!

What does such a thing look like in practice and how does one go about creating it? Simply declaring a space as "intentionally brave" and explaining to folks in the room a requirement for them to consciously, willfully, and intentionally bring qualities such a courage, vulnerability, patience, and empathy can be enough. With that said, an additional step of co-creating some rules for the room can encourage commitment and ensure that the way is paved for the types of behavior that will facilitate the types of conversations that lead to the desired impacts. There is a myriad of beautiful ways to do this, but the simplest method I employ goes like this:

- Briefly introduce the topic of psychological safety (as outlined in Chapter 1).

- Invite each member of the group to write down qualities they would like to be both present in and missing from the room to enable the experience of psychological safety.

- Ask each person to read out one of their qualities in turn while they are written up on a (virtual or physical) flip chart. Guide the individuals in the group to not offer any duplicates.

- Keep working through the group one by one until each unique quality has been shared, and facilitate a conversation around any questions.

- Finally, ask the group by show of hands if they are (a) *able* to bring each of the qualities into the room and (b) *willing* to bring each of the qualities in the room.

- As a final touch, if the group is in the same physical space as each other,[64] I will invite each person to place their signature on the flip chart where I have recorded the qualities. I find that this tends to "seal the deal" in terms of commitment to the intentionally brave space.

Safe rooms are no less brave, but they are different in terms of who is in the room. Safe rooms are not necessarily a new concept, but I have seen them emerge in professional spaces in 2020 in response to the killings of George Floyd, Breonna Taylor, and Ahmaud Arbery as a way for their Black employees to process and share their thoughts and fears and to be heard in ways that they usually don't get to be heard in the professional environment.

---

[64] The early 2020s have presented some wonderful opportunities to get creative with extended shelter-in-place orders in effect around the world due to the COVID-19 pandemic.

To that end, safe rooms work best when they are facilitated for a specific community by someone from that community with those from outside the community able to join in a listening or watching capacity only.[65]

They are not easy experiences to run, participate in, or observe but often have a profound impact. Here's what one participant shared about her recent experience:

> Thank you so much for coming out to support us! In light of everything happening and that has happened, I needed some time to sit with my thoughts. The Safe Room for Black Women was a program I didn't know I needed until I was fully immersed in it. It provided the resources and the space I needed to share, learn, and grow, not only on a personal level, but a professional one as well.

I have likely not included *everything* that will lead to a fully inclusive workplace. Given the complexity of human identity, the work that companies can do to facilitate diversity and inclusion is ever evolving and never complete.

---

[65] PSA: The potential for the presence of spectators to make a safe room feel like a spectacle is significant. If the safe room is to include people who are watching/listening, it is crucial that the facilitator take action to ensure that this feels safe for the participants and to ensure that the nondominant group participants' pain is not being misused by the dominant group.

With that said, the considerations I've laid out herein will, if implemented, provide a strong and sure platform upon which companies can feel assured that they will have gone to good lengths to create the conditions in which the experience of belonging for its employees is in reach and is a real possibility.

A STORY OF INCLUSION

GH is a white, straight, cisgender male who lives in Southern California.

IN MY OPINION, BELONGING IS THE EXTENT TO WHICH we do or don't feel safe and supported to be ourselves.

When I first started working at a gym in my community, years ago, one of the owners and a leader in the company paid little to no attention to me while clearly giving much more attention to others. This pattern of "favoritism" has been toxic in my workplace experience. I was a new trainer coming in to a respected and well-established community, and I was very nervous and sensitive to how others were behaving around me. Not having a full sense of belonging increased my feelings of insecurity, doubt, and shame.

In this state, I felt much less open, authentic, and safe to be fully myself.

Now, however, I've worked at a CrossFit gym for the past twelve years, and there's a certain joy of community that can be experienced there. Whenever I enter the space and see smiles and welcoming gestures like "hello" and "good morning," I feel more belonging and connection. Yesterday, a friend was curious about what my partner and I are going to name our baby. The warmth I felt between us during that conversation stimulated in me a certain sense of belonging in the space. Getting to know and spending time with the folks of this community creates a foundation to connect and feel safety/belonging. After this conversation, I felt much more at ease. I had listened to the best of my ability to my friend, and I was able to show up with my voice as well, expressing myself authentically. I noticed that I felt more present and at ease the rest of the morning. It was a nice way to start the day.

As this chapter ends, I would like to offer the following conclusions:

- **Inclusivity is important.** It is only by making diversity a fact *and* instilling inclusive behaviors in your workplace that belonging can exist.

- **Behavior matters.** Workplace microaggressions and trauma are another fact in most organizations. Instead of denying that they have occurred, do the work of creating safe rooms and intentionally brave spaces to help your employees call in and process these occurrences—and work toward a more inclusive workplace.

- *Your* **behavior matters too.** By learning to go from bystander to up-stander, from ally to accomplice, you model inclusive behaviors and demonstrate what you expect from those around you.

By now, you have addressed diversity and learned to facilitate inclusion. With both of these in place, your organization has its best chance of creating a culture that supports a sense of belonging—for everyone.

CONCLUSION

As part of my master's degree, I was sitting in a class that was being taught by a professor named Rachel Vaughan. In the middle of the class, I realized—out of the blue, like a slap to the face, immobilizing me—that because of the body I walk around in, to some people I will never be a safe space.

Even though I am part of a marginalized community, I still have aspects of my identity that come with privilege.

Because of the years of social oppression, marginalization, and legislation that has done harm to certain communities, because of interpersonal violence as well as violence at the hands of the system—because I am white, and because I walk around this planet in a male body, no matter who I think I am or how I think about myself—I am still going to represent something undesirable to some people.

When I had that realization, I felt ashamed. I felt guilty and helpless, like I was coming undone.

I sat with that and worked on it—and as a direct result of that insight, and the learning that followed, the path I took in going into my own therapy, in engaging in my own personal education to keep my own cultural humility, I had a new realization: while I cannot do anything about the privilege I have been born with, I can do something with it.

I can demonstrate that I am a safe space by taking account of my identity and being aware of it when I am in spaces where there are people who don't look like me.

PUT ON YOUR OWN OXYGEN MASK BEFORE YOU CAN HELP OTHERS

As a direct result of that learning, and that path I took after that slap to the face, I have curated a curriculum of learning that goes beyond unconscious bias training to explore topics of identity, privilege, and fragility[66] and brings the topic of social

---

[66] Robin DiAngelo first coined the term "white fragility" in 2011 to describe any defensive instincts or reactions that a white person experiences when questioned about race or made to consider their own race. Since then, the term has expanded to be used in other areas of oppression (e.g., "straight fragility" and "male fragility").

justice into the workplace through the creation of carefully held, intentionally brave spaces where meaningful conversation and exploration can take place.

This training draws on my experience of working in community mental health and spaces that center social justice as a mental health issue. It consists of a series of four-hour workshops that are based around the idea of flying a plane.

When you board, the safety announcement tells you that in the event of the air pressure in the cabin dropping, masks will fall from the ceiling. And they tell you to put your own mask on first, before helping others. This program is a way of putting on your own oxygen mask and exploring the issues of identity, intersectionality, and privilege from your own perspective, so that you learn from a lived, personal experience first, and so that you're not learning about it as a theoretical concept. I am helping people to become more aware of who they are so that they can move around the world in an inclusive way and with more consciousness about how their identity impacts other people, even before they've opened their mouth or done anything, just by walking into the room.

A flight has a takeoff, a pinnacle, and then it has a landing, so I've structured the program to provide for a gentle takeoff, an enjoyable flight, and a gentle landing.

- In the first workshop, the takeoff, we discuss definitions, concepts, and some history.

- In the second workshop, I get people to reflect on their intersectional identity, who they are, how do they know that's who they are, and the social conditioning that has led them to be the "them" that they are today.

- During the third workshop, we watch short videos that are quite evocative on the topics of race, gender, and the queer community, and perspectives from people from those communities that show what life is like for them. Once people have watched those movies, they go into discussion groups and talk about the thoughts and feelings that came up for them as they watched.

- In the fourth workshop, when we're coming down to land, we get into the space of our own projections and biases, our inner critic. Then when we land the plane, the gentle landing is consolidating our learning and making commitments to inclusion.

I have also curated a list of resources—books, Instagram accounts, TED Talks, movies, podcasts, and articles—that are all aimed at helping people continue their journey of self-discovery, to become more self-aware and, in doing so, become more *other*-aware. All in the name of helping people develop their inner (and outer) social justice warrior.

Since 2018, I have had the fortune to run this curriculum with corporate teams in New Delhi, London, Minneapolis, New York, San Francisco, Seattle, Singapore, Toronto, and Tokyo. I share here a couple of quotes from participants by way of demonstrating its impact:[67]

> "This training is a wonderful example of
> how companies can take responsibility for the
> big picture and investing resources in educating our
> talent on the important matters of diversity that
> affect all of us in one way or another.
> The training had a notable impact on me both
> in my personal life and in the way I relate to my
> colleagues in the office: it empowered me to
> be braver and more empathetic in building
> closer connections with others."
>
> —GJ, a German, straight, white, cisgender,
> able-bodied female

---

[67] If you are interested in running this workshop series with your team or if you would like to discuss a more bespoke learning experience and/or consulting, please contact me at dds@soultrained.com.

"It's the best training I have done in my life.
It touched me in my soul. It opened my eyes on the way
I see and approach relationships and interactions
with others. It helped me to get a better understanding of
my own identity so that I can have greater empathy
for the experience and identities of others and
the sometimes terrible things humans
have to endure on the daily."

—VB, a British, straight, mixed-race,
cisgender, able-bodied male

"I thought diversity and inclusion were Western issues.
How wrong was I?"

—FH, a Singaporean, straight,
cisgender, able-bodied female

"It was an eye-opening and informative experience,
even if it was uncomfortable about 100 percent of the time!
This is the exact type of training all employees should
participate in. To have conversations that you don't normally
have at work but are needed. It will ensure that I'm
continually thinking about the world from many views
and be the inclusive filter that this world needs."

—RM, an American, queer, Black,
cisgender female who uses a wheelchair

Because of my experiences working with these diverse groups of people, I learned the power of shutting up. I became aware of how much I spoke in rooms, and I became increasingly aware of the subtleties of my behavior.

There was a moment a few years ago when I was facilitating an executive offsite and I had a group of executives standing at a flip chart doing some work. In a split second, I became aware that I was about to hand the pen to the only female in the group, so that she could be the scribe.

In that moment, I stopped. Then I gave the pen to the most senior man and asked him to be the note-taker instead.

Recognizing and becoming aware of the behaviors that have been socially conditioned within me doesn't make me a bad person; it makes me a product of my conditioning. *However,* I believe it is all of our jobs to become more aware of that social conditioning so that we can reprogram, bring about more equity, and facilitate more belonging. The job of unlearning your social conditioning is never going to be done. You can't go on a course and receive a sticker that says, "Congratulations! You are woke."

It is an ongoing process of unlearning and relearning how to be a human. First, to become aware of the social conditioning you've been subjected to, and then to learn to dismantle your own internalized racism, heterosexism, sexism, ableism, colorism, and whatever our societal conditions have taught is good versus bad, right versus wrong. Unlearning that is our job.

And when we all make this learning and unlearning our jobs, workplaces become enlivening places where people perform at their best. What's more, they *want* to be there, because when you belong somewhere, you look forward to being there. That place of belonging is so compelling for us. When we find somewhere we belong, we *will* keep going back.

THIS IS NECESSARY NOW

Let's be real: right now, the veil is being lifted. Whatever your political persuasion, it is an inescapable reality that in the latter half of the 2010s and on, the number of hate crimes against marginalized communities increased.

Because of social media and the ability for people to record and share, this history of racial crimes and crimes against the LGBTQIA2+ community has a greater spotlight shined upon it. It's not that this wasn't happening before 2016—racism, heterosexism, and discrimination are certainly not new—but there has been an uptick. And what *is* new is the awareness of how many instances of this hatred occur every moment of every day. (And then, of course, we have COVID, which has further exacerbated race crimes against the Asian American and Pacific Islander community.)

The attention that the murder of George Floyd received globally became a nexus point. It made industry sit up and listen in a way it previously hadn't.

The hate crimes, the heinous and grievous acts, and the emergence of cancel culture—the world of business has responded in the 2020s in a way they weren't responding in the 1990s, 2000s, and 2010s.

That's what's happening *now*.

We are having a national and *global* uncovering of all these things that we were previously forced to keep quiet and hidden. The 2020s have been a process of uncovering, of lifting the veil, and of people responding. The conversation now isn't just about diversity; it's about inclusion, equity, and, instead of making people feel othered, helping them to feel that they belong.

As this continues, we will realize that instead of our differences being problematic, they are *essential*.

We are currently living in a world where our differences are a source of divergence, of othering, where it is us versus them. But it is possible to create a place where our differences are synergistic, greater than the sum of their parts, and where they are absolutely crucial to our success (not a blocker to it) —individually, relationally, on a community level, nationally, and globally.

This is bigger than any one person or even any one company— and it's what's possible when belonging becomes the norm instead of the new.

IT STARTS WITH YOU

The first steps start with you.

When you are in charge of some part of the workplace dynamic and infrastructure—whether you are a founder, CEO, chief talent officer, leader, or manager—you are not going to be able to achieve an inclusive workplace where people experience belonging if you don't do your own work.

A really quick way to become increasingly self-aware in the spirit of becoming increasingly other-aware is to check who you follow on your social media channels. Just think about the amount of time we spend doom-scrolling. You're at home, watching *Survivor* season forty on TV, and there's a particularly fraught moment in the tribal council. Don't you pick up your phone and start scrolling so you don't have to engage with that anxiety-inducing scene. No? Just me?

This scrolling has become an inescapable aspect of our lifestyle, whether it's the first thing we do in the morning, the last thing we do at night, or what we do while we're on the toilet. It is feeding us messages all the time—but we get to select who we follow. Are you following people who affirm your privilege, or are you following people who challenge it?

One of the quickest ways to start shifting your perspective around diversity, inclusion, and belonging is by educating yourself around who you follow on social media.

It is important to remember that it is not the job of a member of a marginalized or historically disempowered or underrepresented group to teach us about their experience. We have to do our own education. We don't go onto social media to ask a Black person why we can't touch their hair or walk up to a trans person and ask what bottom surgery is like. You just don't do that. That person has experienced enough harm at the hands of the system; they don't need to experience additional harm for the purposes of our education. We have Google for that. We have books we can read, videos we can watch, and podcasts we can listen to.

You are in a position of power. And while looking inward is an individual experience, you have the opportunity to take this larger than yourself.

There are three steps to take on your journey from self-aware to other-aware:

1. Reflection

2. Education

3. Implementation

This book includes places to reflect, an education that's being given, and tools that can be implemented—but this is just the beginning.

This is your pocket guide, not your encyclopedia. This is your thought catalyst, a place where you can seek inspiration. It's the place you start, not the place you end.

We've come to the end of the book, but this is just the beginning of your journey.

APPENDIX

RESOURCES

READING

A Race Is a Nice Thing to Have: A Guide to Being a White Person or Understanding the White Persons in Your Life by Janet E Helms

Aria: A Memoir of a Bilingual Childhood by Richard Rodriguez

Becoming a Man: The Story of a Transition by P. Carl

Between the World and Me by Ta-Nehisi Coates

Borderlands / La Frontera: The New Mestiza by Gloria E. Anzaldúa

Caste: The Origins of Our Discontents by Isabel Wilkerson

Child of the Moon by Jessica Semaan

Delusions of Gender: How Our Minds, Society, and Neurosexism Create Difference by Cordelia Fine

Emergent Strategy: Shaping Change, Changing Worlds by Adrienne Maree Brown

Healing Resistance: A Radically Different Response to Harm by Kazu Haga

Here for It: Or, How to Save Your Soul in America by R. Eric Thomas

Fish Cheeks by Amy Tan

My Grandmother's Hands: Racialized Trauma and the Pathway to Mending Our Hearts and Bodies by Resmaa Menakem

Post Traumatic Slave Syndrome: America's Legacy of Enduring Injury and Healing by Dr. Joy DeGruy

Seeing Gender: An Illustrated Guide to Identity and Expression by Iris Gottlieb

So You Want to Talk About Race by Ijeoma Oluo

The 57 Bus: A True Story of Two Teenagers and the Crime That Changed Their Lives by Dashka Slater

The Dark Fantastic: Race and the Imagination from Harry Potter to the Hunger Games by Ebony Elizabeth Thomas

The Hate U Give by Angie Thomas

The New Jim Crow: Mass Incarceration in the Age of Colorblindness by Michelle Alexander

This Bridge Called My Back: Radical Writings from Women of Color edited by Cherríe Moraga and Gloria Anzaldúa

White Fragility: Why It's So Hard for White People to Talk About Racism by Robin DiAngelo

White Supremacy and Me: Combat Racism, Change the World, and Become a Good Ancestor by Layla F. Saad

LISTENING

1619—Nikole-Hannah Jones, the *New York Times*

Call Your Girlfriend: Use the Power You Have—Aminatou Sow, Ann Friedman, and Gina Delvac

Hidden Brain: A Conversation About Life's Unseen Patterns, "'Man Up': How a Fear of Appearing Feminine Restricts Men, and Affects Us All"—Shankar Vedantam, Parth Shah, Tara Boyle, and Rhaina Cohen, NPR

Nice White Parents—Chana Joffe-Walt, the *New York Times*

Scene on Radio: Seeing White—John Biewen, Center for Documentary Studies at Duke University

Scene on Radio: MEN—John Biewen and Celeste Headlee, Center for Documentary Studies at Duke University

Scene on Radio: The Land That Has Never Been Yet—John Biewen and Chenjerai Kumanyika, Center for Documentary Studies at Duke University

WATCHING

13th, Ava DuVernay

America Son, Kenny Leon

Beautiful Thing, Hettie MacDonald

BlacKkKlansman, Spike Lee

Blue Is the Warmest Color, Abdellatif Kechiche

Booksmart, Olivia Wilde

Boy Erased, Joel Edgerton

Boys Don't Cry, Kimberly Peirce

But I'm a Cheerleader, Jamie Babbit

Call Me by Your Name, Luca Guadagnino

CBQM, Dennis Allen

Dear White People, Justin Simien, 2017–2021

Hannah Gadsby: Douglas, Hannah Gadsby, Madeleine Perry

God's Own Country, Frances Lee

I Am, Tom Shadyac

My Beautiful Laundrette, Stephen Frears

Moonlight, Barry Jenkins

Hannah Gadsby: Nanette, by Hannah Gadsby, Madeleine Perry

Paris Is Burning, Jennie Livingston

Pariah, Dee Rees

POSE, Ryan Murphy, Brad Falchuk, Steven Canals, 2018–2021

Pride, Matthew Warchus

Sex Education, Laurie Nunn, 2019–Ongoing

The Hate U Give, George Tillman Jr.

The Mask You Live In, Jennifer Siebel Newsom

"The Village," by Wrabel

Two Spirits: Sexuality, Gender, and the Murder of Fred Martinez, Lydia Nibley

"White Savior: The Movie Trailer," Late Night with Seth Meyers

Visible: Out on Television, Ryan White

SOCIAL

@actuallyautisticadvocate

@adriennemareebrown

@allyhenny

@alokvmenon

@antiracismdaily

@bl.ack.magic.wo.man

@ckyourprivilege

@decolonizemyself

@diversifyournarrative

@gayglossary

@harnaamkaur

@ihartericka

@jake_graf5

@laylafsaad

@lgbt_history

@nowhitesaviors

@openheartwellnesscollective

@outmagazine

@pink_news

@queerconscious

@shityoushouldcareabout

@soyouwanttotalkabout

@sonyareneetaylor

@theaidsmemorial

@them

@thenapministry

@yourdiagnonsense

@together.rising

BIBLIOGRAPHY

American Psychological Association. "Stress in America 2020 Survey Signals a Growing National Mental Health Crisis." American Psychological Association. October 20, 2020. https://www.apa.org/news/press/releases /2020/10/stress-mental-health-crisis.

Baker, Kellan, Laura E. Durso, and Aaron Ridings. "How to Collect Data About LGBT Communities." Center for American Progress. March 15, 2016. https:// www.americanprogress.org/issues/lgbtq-rights/reports/2016/03/15/133223/ how-to-collect-data-about-lgbt-communities/.

Bastian, Rebekah. "How to Foster Workplace Belonging Through Successful Employee Resource Groups." *Forbes*, February 11, 2019. https://www.forbes. com/sites/rebekahbastian/2019/02/11/how-to-foster-workplace-belong ing-through-successful-employee-resource-groups/?sh=42977e09dc73.

Baume, Matt. "Trump Administration Moves Closer to Allowing Hospitals to Turn Away Queer Patients." *Them*, April 25, 2020. https://www.them.us/story /trump-administration-moves-closer-to-allowing-hospitals-to-turn-away -queer-patients.

Baumeister, Roy F., and Mark R. Leary. "The Need to Belong: Desire for Interpersonal Attachments as a Fundamental Human Motivation."

Psychological Bulletin 117, no. 3 (1995): 497–529. https://doi.org/10.1037/0033
-2909.117.3.497.

Beard, Alison, and Curt Nickisch. "Real Leaders: Oprah Winfrey and the Power
of Empathy." Produced by *Harvard Business Review*. *HBR Ideacast*. March
26, 2020. Podcast, MP3 audio, 29:09. https://hbr.org/podcast/2020/03/real
-leaders-oprah-winfrey-and-the-power-of-empathy.

Bedarkar, Madhura, and Deepika Pandita. "A Study on the Drivers of Employee
Engagement Impacting Employee Performance." *Procedia - Social and
Behavioral Sciences* 133, (2014): 106–115.

Bennis, Warren G. *Organization Development: Its Nature, Origins, and Prospects*.
Boston: Addison-Wesley, 1969.

Bethea, Aiko. "What Black Employee Resource Groups Need Right Now."
Harvard Business Review, June 29, 2020. https://hbr.org/2020/06/what
-black-employee-resource-groups-need-right-now.

Biewen, John. *Scene on Radio*. Podcast audio. 2015–2021. sceneonradio.org.

Bowlby, John. *A Secure Base: Parent-Child Attachment and Healthy Human
Development*. Oxford: Routledge, 1988.

Boyers, Jayson. "Why Empathy Is the Force That Moves Business Forward."
Forbes, May 30, 2013. https://www.forbes.com/sites/ashoka/2013/05/30/why
-empathy-is-the-force-that-moves-business-forward/?sh=c2bd3a5169e5.

Brief, Arthur P., and Howard M. Weiss. "Organizational Behavior: Affect in the
Workplace." *Annual Review of Psychology* 53, no. 1 (2002): 279–307. https://doi
.org/10.1146/annurev.psych.53.100901.135156.

Brown, Brené. "The Power of Vulnerability." TEDx Houston. June 2010. https:
//www.ted.com/talks/brene_brown_the_power_of_vulnerability?language
=en.

Buckingham, Marcus, and Curt Coffman. *First, Break All the Rules: What the
World's Greatest Managers Do Differently*. New York: Simon & Schuster, 1999.

Carless, Sally A. "Does Psychological Empowerment Mediate the Relationship Between Psychological Climate and Job Satisfaction?" *Journal of Business and Psychology* 18, (2004): 405–425. https://doi.org/10.1023/B:JOBU.0000028 444.77080.c5.

Clark, Timothy. *The 4 Stages of Psychological Safety: Defining the Path to Inclusion and Innovation.* Oakland, CA: Berrett-Koehler Publishers, 2020.

Commission for Architecture and the Built Environment. *Inclusion by Design: Equality, Diversity and the Built Environment.* London: CABE, 2008. https:// www.designcouncil.org.uk/sites/default/files/asset/document/inclusion -by-design.pdf.

Covey, Stephen R. *The 7 Habits of Highly Effective People: Restoring the Character Ethic.* Boston: G. K. Hall & Co, 1997.

deVilla, Joey. "Requiring Eight Years Experience for a Junior Position Is Ridiculous (Or: How to Get a Job, Part 1)." *Global Nerdy* (blog). May 10, 2020. https://www.globalnerdy.com/2020/05/10/requiring-eight-years-experience -for-a-junior-position-is-ridiculous-or-how-to-get-a-job-part-1/.

Dobson-Smith, D. P. (DDS). "The Need to Belong." LinkedIn, September 4, 2019. https://www.linkedin.com/pulse/need-belong-daniel-dobson-smith/.

Dwoskin, Elizabeth. "Americans Might Never Come Back to the Office, and Twitter Is Leading the Charge." *The Washington Post*, October 1, 2020. https://www .washingtonpost.com/technology/2020/10/01/twitter-work-from-home/?arc 404=true.

Eliot, Lise. "Neurosexism: The Myth That Men and Women Have Different Brains." *Nature*, February 27, 2019. https://www.nature.com/articles/d41586 -019-00677-x.

Fraley, Chris R. "Adult Attachment Theory and Research: A Brief Overview." R. Chris Fraley.com. 2018. http://labs.psychology.illinois.edu/~rcfraley/ attachment.htm.

Freud, Sigmund. *Civilization and Its Discontents.* New York: W. W. Norton & Company, 1989.

Goffee, Robert, and Gareth Jones. *Why Should Anyone Be Led by You? What It Takes to Be an Authentic Leader.* Brighton, MA: HBR Press, 2006.

Goleman, Daniel, Richard Boyatzis, and Annie McKee. *The New Leaders: Transforming the Art of Leadership into the Science of Results.* London: Little, Brown Book Group, 2002.

Google. "Guide: Understand Team Effectiveness." re:Work. September 7, 2020. https://rework.withgoogle.com/print/guides/5721312655835136/.

Hopkins, Walt. "I'm a Straight White Guy—So What's Diversity Got to Do With Me?" In *The Reading Book for Human Relations Training,* edited by Alfred L. Cooke, Michael Brazzel, Argentine Saunders Craig, and Barbara Greig, 8th ed. Silver Spring, MA: NTL Publications, 1999. 121–126.

Kahn, William A. "Psychological Conditions of Personal Engagement and Disengagement at Work." *Academy of Management Journal* 33, no. 4 (1990): 692–724. https://doi.org/10.5465/256287.

Katz, Jonathan N. *The Invention of Heterosexuality.* Chicago: University of Chicago Press, 2014.

Kimmel, Michael S., and Abby L. Ferber. *Privilege: A Reader.* 4th ed. Boulder: Westview Press, 2017.

Knight, Rebecca. "7 Practical Ways to Reduce Bias in Your Hiring Process: Start by Reworking Your Job Descriptions." SHRM. April 19, 2018. https://www.shrm.org/resourcesandtools/hr-topics/talent-acquisition/pages/7-practical-ways-to-reduce-bias-in-your-hiring-process.aspx.

Kohut, Heinz. *The Analysis of the Self: A Systematic Approach to the Psychoanalytic Treatment of Narcissistic Personality Disorders.* Chicago: The University of Chicago Press, 1971.

Kohut, Heinz, and Ernest S. Wolf. "The Disorders of the Self and Their Treatment: An Outline." *The International Journal of Psychoanalysis* 59, no. 4 (1978): 413–425.

Kolbert, Elizabeth. "There's No Scientific Basis for Race—It's a Made-Up Label." *National Geographic*, March 12, 2018. https://www.nationalgeographic.com/magazine/2018/04/race-genetics-science-africa/.

Kottler, Amanda. "Feeling at Home, Belonging, and Being Human: Kohut, Self Psychology, Twinship, and Alienation." *International Journal of Psychoanalytic Self Psychology* 10, no. 4 (2015): 378–389. https://doi.org/10.1080/15551024.2015.1074000.

Kruse, Kevin. "Are You Engaged at Work? The Importance of Friendship and Employee Resource Groups." *Forbes*, September 29, 2014. https://www.forbes.com/sites/kevinkruse/2014/09/29/employee-resource-groups-ergs-employee-engagement/?sh=5369d9011bd7

Lambert, Nathaniel M., Tyler F. Stillman, Joshua A. Hicks, Shanmukh Kamble, Roy F. Baumeister, and Frank D. Fincham. "To Belong Is to Matter: Sense of Belonging Enhances Meaning in Life." *Personality and Social Psychology Bulletin* 39, no. 11 (2013): 1418–1427. https://doi.org/10.1177/0146167213499186.

Markos, Solomon, and M. Sandhya Sridevi. "Employee Engagement: The Key to Improving Performance." *International Journal of Business and Management* 5, no. 12 (2010): 89–96. https://doi.org/10.5539/ijbm.v5n12p89.

Maslow, Abraham H. "A Theory of Human Motivation." *Psychological Review* 50, no. 4 (1943): 370–396. https://doi.org/10.1037/h0054346.

McClure, John P., and James M. Brown. "Belonging at Work." *Human Resource Development International* 11, no. 1 (2008): 3–17. https://doi.org/10.1080/13678860701782261.

Mead, Elaine. "5 Ridiculous 'Requirements' I Wish Employers Would Drop from Job Ads." *Medium*, April 27, 2020. https://medium.com/swlh/5-ridiculous-requirements-i-wish-employers-would-drop-from-job-ads-b965fded2c4d.

Mitchell, Stephen A., and Margaret J. Black. *Freud and Beyond: A History of Modern Psychoanalytic Thought.* New York: Basic Books, 2016.

O'Donnell, Michael. "Ridiculous Job Descriptions Chase Away Some of the Best Candidates." LinkedIn, December 10, 2018. https://www.linkedin.com/pulse/ ridiculous-job-descriptions-chase-away-some-best-michael-o-donnell/.

Reid, David. "Almost 40% of the World's Countries Will Witness Civil Unrest in 2020, Research Claims." CNBC. January 16, 2020. https://www.cnbc. com/2020/01/16/40percent-of-countries-will-witness-civil-unrest-in-2020 -report-claims.html.

Remling, Jennifer, and Joe Remling. *Carve Your Own Road: Do What You Love and Live the Life You Envision.* Wayne, NJ: Career Press, 2009.

Rodman, Robert F. *Winnicott: His Life and Work.* Lebanon, IN: Da Capo Lifelong Books, 2004.

Rodríguez-Rey, Rocío, Helena Garrido-Hernansaiz, and Silvia Collado. "Psychological Impact and Associated Factors During the Initial Stage of the Coronavirus (COVID-19) Pandemic Among the General Population in Spain." *Frontiers in Psychology* 11, (2020): 1540. https://doi.org/10.3389/ fpsyg.2020.01540.

RSA. "Brené Brown on Empathy." YouTube. December 10, 2013. Video, 2:53. https: //www.youtube.com/watch?v=1Evwgu369Jw&t=2s.

Savage, Maddy. "Coronavirus: The Possible Long-term Mental Health Impacts." *BBC.* October 28, 2020. https://www.bbc.com/worklife/article/20201021 -coronavirus-the-possible-long-term-mental-health-impacts.

Schulner, David, Y. Shireen Razack, and Eric Manheimer, writers. *New Amsterdam.* Season 2, episode 16, "Perspectives." Directed by Craig Zisk, featuring Ryan Eggold, Janet Montgomery, and Freema Agyeman. Aired March 10, 2020. NBC.

Siegel, Allen M. *Heinz Kohut and the Psychology of the Self.* Oxford: Routledge, 2008.

Sinek, Simon. *Leaders Eat Last: Why Some Teams Pull Together and Others Don't.* New York: Portfolio, 2017.

Sinek, Simon. "What Empathy Looks Like | Simon Sinek." YouTube. August 11, 2020. Video, 1:21. https://www.youtube.com/watch?v=tfWC9IsoGyQ.

Soll, Jack B., Katherine L. Milkman, and John W. Payne. "Outsmart Your Own Biases: How to Broaden Your Thinking and Make Better Decisions." *Harvard Business Review*, May 2015. https://hbr.org/2015/05/outsmart-your-own-biases.

Sugrue, Thomas J. "2020 Is Not 1968: To Understand Today's Protests, You Must Look Further Back." *National Geographic*, June 11, 2020. https://www.national geographic.com/history/2020/06/2020-not-1968/#close.

"The Theory." Center for Self-Determination Theory. Accessed October 8, 2021. https://selfdeterminationtheory.org/the-theory/.

Transgender Law Center. *Model Transgender Employment Policy: Negotiating for Inclusive Workspaces.* Oakland, CA: Transgender Law Center, 2020. http://transgenderlawcenter.org/wp-content/uploads/2013/12/model-work place-employment-policy-Updated1.pdf.

Tschudy, Ted. "On Being in the Privileged Position: Things My Parents Couldn't Teach Me." In *The Reading Book for Human Relations Training*, edited by Alfred L. Cooke, Michael Brazzel, Argentine Saunders Craig, and Barbara Greig, 8th ed. Silver Spring, MA: NTL Publications, 1999. 143–147.

Valentine, Brittany. "Menstruation products belong in all bathrooms." *The Temple News*, November 12, 2019. https://temple-news.com/menstruation -products-belong-in-all-bathrooms/.

Wrzesniewski, Amy. "Finding Positive Meaning in Work." In *Positive Organizational Scholarship: Foundations of a New Discipline*, edited by Kim S. Cameron, Jane E. Dutton, and Robert E. Quinn, 296–308. Oakland, CA: Berrett-Koehler Publishers, 2003.

ABOUT ME

I am a queer, nonbinary, non-disabled, white British immigrant, who was assigned male at birth, and I have lived in the US with my husband, David, since 2014. I love the California sunshine, geeking out about psychology, and like to lose myself by watching repeats of *The Voice* and *X-Factor* on YouTube.

I have notched up more than twenty years of working in small, medium, and large corporations. I literally grew up in the hospitality industry (my parents owned a pub and restaurant in the UK), and I started my career as a college professor teaching hotel and business management. I've since held a range of senior, executive, and C-suite-level roles across a host of sectors and companies, including retailer Marks & Spencer Plc, travel and tourism company Eurostar International, Crossrail Ltd (the company charged with building a new railway through the center of London), music giant Sony Music Entertainment, and Essence Global, which is part of the world's largest advertising company, WPP. These roles have provided the opportunity for me to work across all continents and to develop the awareness and empathy required to work successfully with people from all walks of life and diverse backgrounds.

Before I moved to the US in 2014, I managed a small psychotherapy private practice as a registered neuro-linguistic psychotherapist. Neuro-linguistic psychotherapy (NLPt) has its roots in a body of work known as neuro-linguistic programming (NLP) which was founded in the seventies by Richard Bandler (a mathematician, computer programmer, and therapist) and John Grinder (a world-renowned linguist).

Bandler and Grinder were heavily influenced by the Human Potential Movement and by Gregory Bateson (anthropologist, social scientist, linguist, and systems thinker), Fritz and Laura Perls (the founders of Gestalt psychotherapy), Virginia Satir (family therapist), and Milton Erickson (psychiatrist, family therapist, and founding president of the American Society for Clinical Hypnosis). While NLPt certainly developed from this body of work, NLPt practitioners trace the roots of the field even further back to Alfred Korzybski's notion that "the map is not the territory," to George Kelly's Psychology of Personal

Constructs, and to the work of George A. Miller, the cognitive scientist.

I'm certified as an executive coach by both the Chartered Institute of Personnel and Development and the Oxford School of Coaching & Mentoring. I'm credentialed with the International Coach Federation, and I am a coach-supervisor through the Coaching Supervision Academy. In 2018, I founded Soul Trained, an executive coaching and leadership growth consultancy.

Through 2020, I spent a year working at Pacific Center for Human Growth in Berkley, the country's second oldest community mental health clinic serving the needs of the LGBTQIA2+ community, which centers mental health as a social justice issue. Through my work at Pacific Center I learned to value the question, "What happened to you?" versus wondering, "What's wrong with you?" and to appreciate the many ways in which systemic racism, sexism, ableism, and heterosexism impact our emotional, mental, and physical health.

In addition to my training in the UK, in 2021, I graduated from California Institute of Integral Studies with an MA in integral counseling psychology. As a student of integral counseling psychology, I've had the opportunity to train with, and learn from, many luminaries in the transpersonal field including

Louise Hay, Marianne Williamson, Dr. Patricia Crane, Brant Cortright, Deepak Chopra, and Jason Chan. In 2007, I became a Reiki master and teacher under the guidance of Christina Moore, and in 2020, I began an internship with The Narrative Enneagram.

Today, I am a member of the Bay Area Gestalt Institute (BAGI) which is a unique and diverse community of psychotherapists and associates, rooted in a lineage of Gestalt teachers and practitioners, and committed to living the values we teach. BAGI's mission is to promote healing, aliveness, and authenticity in our communities and society at large by teaching and providing Gestalt psychotherapy.

I bring all of my experiences as a human and my training as a clinician and a coach to show up in my authenticity, genuineness, and truth and to approach my work and my clinical practice in a person-centered, trauma-informed, culturally humble way.